£11.00

D1190503

accounting for research and development

by Dr J. Batty, MCom, ACMA, MBIM, MIPM

accounting for research and development

BUSINESS BOOKS
London

WILLIAM MADISON RANDALL LIBRARY UNC AT WILMINGTON

First published 1976

© JOSEPH BATTY, 1976

*All rights reserved. Except for normal review purposes,
no part of this book may be reproduced or utilised in any
form or by any means, electronic or mechanical, including
photocopying, recording, or by any information storage
and retrieval system, without permission of the publishers.*

ISBN 0 220 66290 2

This book has been set 11 on 12 point IBM Press Roman,
prepared for press by The Ivory Head Press,
170 Murray Road, London W5, and printed in
Great Britain by W & J Mackay Limited, Chatham
by photo-litho for the publishers, Business Books Limited,
24 Highbury Crescent, London N5

CONTENTS

HF5681
.R35
.B37
1976

226357

PREFACE

Research and Development are vital parts of the industrial and commercial scene. Workers involved in these vital functions have to be permitted to operate in an environment that encourages new ideas, products and commercial opportunities to come forward at the opportune time. Managing the vast sums of money involved and having the faith to keep committing a business years into the future requires the exercise of imagination, skill and expertise.

Results can only be measured by reference to revenues, costs and profitability. Admittedly, there are other indicators such as improvement of the conditions and health of mankind, but for a commercial business, these usually have to be relegated to a subsidiary role. Financial planning and accountability must play a considerable part in determining the success or failure of the R&D function.

Many books on the management of R&D make reference to the financial implications. Usually these books are written by non-accountants and deal with the technical problems. Although admirable in themselves they do not present a fully *integrated* approach to the technical and financial implications.

This book shows how R&D can be viewed as a vital corporate function. At the same time, reference is made throughout to the Accounting necessary for implementing a programme as well as for controlling.

No previous knowledge is assumed and, therefore, in this sense the text may be said to be 'introductory'. However, since budgeting, cost accounting, cash management and financial reporting are all explained within the context of R&D. it may be said that a more than normal coverage is attempted.

The intention therefore is to bring together in a basic book the fundamentals of accounting and the management of R&D. The expected readership is accountants, company directors and R&D managers. It is hoped that their needs will be covered by a comprehensive, general work that examines all the main features without delving too deeply into specialised, technical aspects that are applicable to a limited number of practitioners.

J. BATTY

Acknowledgements

I acknowledge the references made (see References and Bibliography for complete details) and the assistance given by many individuals and organisations in preparing this book. My thanks are offered to the following:

The Institute of Chartered Accountants in England and Wales.
National Association of Accountants (USA).
BP Research Centre for details of case study.
The Charpie Report, Hoskins and Sells, New York.
E. D. Reeves, *Management of Industrial Research.*
R. E. Seiler, *Improving the Effectiveness of R&D.*
B. V. Carsberg, *Introduction of Mathematical Programming for Accountants.*
A. Hart, article in *Operational Research Quarterly.*
Management Accounting journal.

1 RESEARCH AND DEVELOPMENT TODAY

1.1 CORPORATE R & D

1.1.1 Scope of study

Research and development is concerned with the *discovery* of new products, methods, services or techniques within a business. Based on the hope of tangible returns that will be greater than the expenditure, considerable sums of money are spent. The degree of success achieved follows no standard pattern. The outcome is uncertain and the risks can be immense; the rewards can also be high.

Accounting for R&D requires that several related problems be dealt with. As a first step it is necessary to define the area to be covered, classifying the costs in a logical and systematic fashion. This should lead to automatic consideration of the time factor — whether costs are to be charged to the period in which they are incurred or carried forward to a subsequent period. If the latter practice is adopted a decision must be made on the proportion to be charged to each accounting year.

The management of R&D, including planning, control and coordination of projects, cannot be isolated from accounting and for this reason, and because accountants should be familiar with the wider issues, reference is made to the economic and managerial aspects. On the other hand, the technical aspects tend to vary from one industry to another and as there are many excellent books and articles on these; in this book explanation of them is kept to a minimum.

There are many difficulties associated with a study of the subject because, where this function is vital to the operations of a company, it will have an impact on other functions or management areas. If new products are developed they must be fitted into the existing production capacity or new factories must be provided. In addition there may be the problem of whether personnel are capable of diversifying into new areas. Any lack of technical knowledge, may mean recruitment of outsiders with the appropriate specialist training and experience. There is also the possible impact on the marketing function; a product should have functional appeal but at the same time it may require certain aesthetic qualities which should be kept in mind during development.

What should be made clear at the start is that no standard definition exists in global terms for the two main parts of R&D:

1   Research.
2   Development.

Usually the two aspects are considered separately both for technical and accounting reasons. However, because of its varied and diverse nature managers in different companies do not necessarily mean the same thing when they speak of 'Research' or 'Development'. Possible definitions are developed later; at this stage it should be apparent that a rigid application is not possible.

The lack of standardisation is not limited to basic definitions. There is a need to recognise the different procedures and practices which exist in industry and commerce. There are different systems of classifying expenditure and then of treating the amounts in the annual accounts and in the costs of products. These differences are reflected in the forms, statements and procedures used within individual companies.

1.1.2   Essentials of the accounting system

Correct accounting is essential, for the following important reasons:

1   There should be a correct record of expenditure incurred on R&D of new products and other activities.
2   The charge made for a particular year will affect the profit reported to shareholders.
3   The method used for classifying exepnditure into *capital* (cost

of producing fixed assets or future benefits) or *revenue*
(operating expenses) can in turn affect the amount of depreciation charged in future periods as well as averaging expenditure
charged from one year to another.
4   Charges in the cost accounts for R&D will affect the costs of
      products and possibly the prices charged to customers.
5   Management decisions for project analysis should be based on
      the full knowledge of the relevant costs relating to the function
      and the possible changes in revenues from the adoption of success-
      ful projects.
6   Financial planning, budgeting, cost control and related activities
      require costs to be classified in a suitable manner.

These and related aspects will be considered in succeeding chapters.

1.2   OVERALL CORPORATE OBJECTIVES

All companies must have objectives, though often these are only implicit in the directors' course of action and are not clearly defined.
These corporate objectives should be understood by all senior personnel and written into some form of policy document. From this it should
be possible to formulate the management philosophy and the general
approach to management problems; in other words, to develop a corporate strategy.
    It is a major problem to persuade many boards of directors and
senior managers to think positively in terms of:

1   What products and services should be produced?
2   Which methods are the most appropriate for their type of
      business?
3   What growth should be expected in terms of sales, profit
      shown as a return on capital employed, and investment in
      plant, equipment and new technologies?

The function has to be integrated within the framework of each
company's corporate strategy. Some companies will spend only a
small amount on R&D, whilst others depend to a large extent upon
innovation for the continued flow of an adequate revenue from new
products and other developments and therefore must have a heavy
commitment.
    Companies will generally break their corporate objectives into long,
medium and short-term aims. The role of the *R&D function* is to
ensure that new ideas and developments are brought forward at the
right time so that the company can continue to operate at least at the

same level of profits and, where the policy is to expand, to allow the expansion to take place as required. In some industries there will be keen competition which makes it essential for R&D to go forward at a fairly rapid pace.

Because of the large expenditure which can result from operating a research centre it is necessary to stipulate the areas of interest in terms of products and services. 'What business to be in?: is a vital question. There should also be the correct balance between long- and short-term objectives, thus allowing developments to be fitted in where convenient, rather than having to be deferred or even lost because they are not commercially viable at the time they are discovered.

Formal planning and control procedures enable all factors that affect R&D to be considered. There must be coordination of projects so that effort is not wasted, and there should be a follow-up to ensure that less successful projects are abandoned and those that have great possibilities are pursued with vigour.

In defining the R&D corporate objectives the board should look at related objectives that cover marketing, purchasing, production, manpower and finance. These will show what results are expected in terms of profitability, contributions and cash flow. The functions cannot operate in a vacuum but should have regard to overall corporate objectives.

1.2.1 Different methods of approach

There are different methods of approach which may be pursued in defining the corporate objectives. Some of the possibilities are:

1 *Leader policy* A company may be regarded as a leader in its field and operate on such a scale that it must pursue large-scale R&D. If this is the case, as occurs with large companies in chemicals, pharmaceuticals and electronics, then a great deal of the corporate thinking will revolve around what is being produced by the project teams. With these companies there is a constant effort made to produce new products, many of which have to be tested for long periods before being marketed. The production of drugs is an excellent example of an R&D-orientated industry.

2 *Imitator policy* There may be a policy of 'following the leaders', waiting for significant break-throughs to occur and then adapting these within the individual company. This approach requires the ability to spot significant developments and then to work on them with great speed so they can be exploited. This method may be adopted by the medium-size company which cannot afford full-scale research facilities.

Obviously the 'leader' companies will do all they can to protect their new products by registering patents and trademarks. However, this is not always easy or practicable; a novel idea may be presented in many different ways.

3   *Restructure policy*   A company may limit its operations to specific areas of investigation which are indicated by particular problems such as the need to create a substitute product or by request from customers who wish specific problems to be solved, for which they are willing to pay. This is more in the nature of *ad hoc* R&D which would not have general application. It would be invaluable for dealing with customers' complaints or other problems.

In practice, it is often found that some form of compromise is the policy adopted, which attempts to achieve an optimum use of resources and commercial exploitation. The factors that influence the decisions to be made are considered in the following sections.

1.2.2   Factors influencing the corporate objectives

In addition to the factors already mentioned, there are other influences that can help to determine how research should be developed and managed. Ideas do not come without effort, or if they do, some means has to be found of channelling them along the appropriate lines so that they can become commercially viable. Precisely how R&D will be organised is considered in a later chapter, but at this stage it is useful to summarise the key factors that affect the size and form of the function:

1   *Management philosophy*   The way a business is managed affects the generation of new ideas. When a company is small, the owner of the business with an inventive turn of mind will look at possible developments and generate new ideas within the constraints laid down by available finance and other factors. Because of the limited reserves, little research work may be carried out, and possibly much of what is done will be on the development of ideas from existing work, or from the research carried out by other companies. Often the reason for the existence of the business is an entrepreneur who is constantly looking for new ideas. If carried out to its fullest extent, this is known as the 'authoritarian style' of management and as the description implies, all drive and direction comes from the top, with little or no scope for initiative from managers. When a company is large, delegation is essential and, therefore, an alternative approach is necessary. The more acceptable style is known as 'participative management', where

6   managers and staff are consulted, and are concerned in the procedures and practices followed within a company. Managers are not consulted on every aspect of policy, but generally the participation extends to the development of better methods of achieving corporate objectives.

In practice in running a business there is usually a combination of participative management and, for some areas, authoritarian management. It will be necessary to indicate the areas to be developed so that personnel do not extend their work beyond what is reasonable for achieving the R&D objectives. The broad framework should be determined by corporate policy approved by the board. Once the R&D personnel know the specific areas to be covered they should be left to work out their ideas on products, methods and other requirements; this freedom on detail may be necessary to obtain the best results. The encouragement of new ideas and techniques is the major problem in development, and if not given, there may be few new ideas for creating new products; this in turn may mean that the business will not keep abreast of current developments and lose ground to competitors.

2   *Keeping abreast of the latest developments*   A company operates within a dynamic environment and information should be available on all the actual and potential changes in marketing, production, computer technology and other areas of interest to the company. Unless a close watch is kept on new developments there could be considerable waste in terms of time, effort and money. As part of this process, it will be necessary to keep in touch with what other companies are doing, the findings in independent research establishments, as well as the work carried out at universities and in government research establishments and departments both in the UK and aboard. The impact of legislation on R&D should also be kept under review, so that new laws can be given full recognition when developing products or services.

3   *Developing an appropriate organisation*   There is no 'ideal' or 'model' organisation structure that can be applied to any company. However, there are many features common to all organisations. The more important of these are now considered:

a   *Effective communications system*   There should be the means of channelling ideas to the manager or committee responsible for authorising expenditure, so that work can proceed. In addition, there is need for a formal system for authorising expenditure, accumulating the cost and, where appropriate, generating action when excess spending has taken place.

b   *Financial control desirable*   In many companies some form of budgetary control system is desirable. Even where a full system is not possible some attempt should be made to plan in advance

how much is to be spent on R&D as a whole, and for individual
projects within the programme.

c *Bases for justification*   When justifying a project, reference
should be made not only to its likely cost or profit, but also its
possible impact on the company as a whole. This approach is vital
because a project viewed in isolation may not show the full
consequences of carrying out the work, especially where new
developments may affect existing products. Moreover, without
proper integration there may be uneconomic use made of the
available resources.

4 Diversifying a company   Diversification is a term that applies
when the existing products appear to have a short life cycle or where
a company wishes to grow to a larger size, or alternatively, where it
is felt that the risks should be spread over a large number of products,
some of which are not necessarily related to the existing products.
There is, therefore, a positive effort made to develop new ideas, products or methods and therefore capture a wider and larger market.

5 Exploiting surplus materials   Again this is a desire to grow or at
least to make full use of potential profitability. It may take the form
of the development of new products when, say, a surplus liquid or gas
is available from the production of an existing product; alternatively,
it may involve concentration on a pool of basic research when it is
recognised that new materials or products could be developed. The
petroleum industry provides examples of new by-products or joint
products developed from oil refining. Products such as nylon, poly-
styrene and transistors have been developed by extending and applying existing theory and technology.

6 Providing for an affluent society   There may be a positive policy
to develop new ideas which are indicated by the changing needs of
society. The affluent society has been criticised on many grounds, but
many new products have been developed because purchasing power has
been available and there has been a desire to keep up appearances in
terms of material wealth. The domestic appliance field is an excellent
example of where products have been developed to meet a new demand.

Conclusion   These are some of the aims or motives that often
influence the amount of R&D thought to be necessary by a particular
company. In themselves they may not be sufficient to justify expenditure at any set level. For the commercial business the prospect of
improving profitability will be the main criterion. There should be
justification directly or indirectly in financial terms, either by looking

at profit, contributions, or some other financial measure such as increase in sales or reduction in costs. Far too many companies are content to accept R&D as necessary without attempting to evaluate the results. This should be done in a systematic way as described later.

1.3   IMPORTANCE OF R&D

The function will vary in importance according to the nature of the specific company. Where the function exists and is carried out in a successful fashion, i.e. where new products and methods are being developed, then there is little doubt that R&D is vital to the company in question. However, the precise reasons for the importance of the function will tend to vary between industries and to some extent between companies within the same industry. The policy followed and the management philosophy can have an important bearing on the question of how important the function is in achieving the corporate objectives.

The division of research into 'basic' and 'applied' can have a bearing in determining how far the R&D function should be developed within a particular company. With 'basic' research little or no apparent benefit may be forthcoming within the short term, but on the other hand, over a longer period it may be evident that many new ideas have come from 'basic' research. The degree to which a company will be concerned with basic research, will depend on company policy and the nature of the industry and its problems. There may be difficulty in some industries in recognising which activities are likely to bring forward practical ideas and for this reason much more time and effort may have to be given to 'basic' research.

In other industries, the areas of operations may be more straightforward and clear cut and for this reason all research can be of an 'applied' nature, concerning specific products, methods, or other new developments.

Bearing in mind the possible differences in approach between companies, some of the aims of R&D are now summarised.

1   Need for a defensive policy   Because of the nature of the industry, such as where there are continual changes in terms of inventions or technical developments, it may be necessary to develop a defensive plan of operation which includes R&D. Put in another way, a company in a highly competitive situation must keep abreast of new ideas to be able to operate successfully. This is a form of 'defensive' R&D; significant developments in the industry have to be countered with some form of defence tactic.

2 Need for an offensive policy When a company looks upon itself
as a leader in a particular field, the policy may be to keep ahead of
competitors and with this purpose as a definite strategy, it sets about
to develop 'offensive' R&D. Any falling off in efficiency will probably
result in loss of the leadership position. Both these aspects are of vital
importance to all companies in a field that relies on innovation.

3 Providing a technical service Some companies specialise in providing a service to customers in the technical, manufacturing or marketing areas so that further sales can be obtained as part of a package or
as a follow on from giving technical advice. The work thus becomes a
specific 'job' for the customer who pays for the work done.

1.4   ANALYSIS OF R&D EXPENDITURE

Many inventions come from small beginnings but there seems little
doubt that the growth of technology to a large extent, is due to
increasing the amount spent on R&D. Many research associations
have grown up in the last decade and are being supplemented by
establishments that are directly controlled by central government.
   As companies have grown in size, especially when multinational
in scope, there has been growth in the amount of research that could
be carried out. This expansion has made it essential to bring forward
new products continuously in order to allow the large company to
operate at an economical size. Multinational companies are now controlled from all the major industrial countries, including the USA,
Holland, Japan and Great Britain. In many cases R&D has been developed at a central point with the benefits extending to all countries
in which the company is operating.
   In the UK around £1000 million is spent annually on the R&D
function, though this figure does not include the substantial amount
spent on North Sea Oil development work for which figures are not
available at the time of writing. This represents approximately 3 per cent
cent of the gross national product and is, therefore, the third highest
rate in the world, the first two places being held by the USA and the
USSR respectively.

1.5   COSTS IN THE INDIVIDUAL COMPANY

R&D costs will vary according to the nature of the business and its
size in terms of capital employed and sales revenue. In many companies there is often a distinct correlation between the amount
spent on the function and the sales achieved. From study of the

published accounts of major R&D-oriented companies, it appears that about 3 per cent of turnover is spent on the development of new products. There were exceptions — a computing company spending approximately 12 per cent — but the smaller figure may be regarded as being more typical.

As shown later, when planning an R&D department, reference should be made to how much a company can afford each year, including a study of the cash flow. There may often appear to be adequate finance, but on a more detailed examination, it may be found that at certain times there is more to be paid out than there is coming in. If problems are to be avoided, any likely cash-flow deficiencies should be forecast before determining how far a company can commit itself to R&D expenditure.

1.5.1   Estimating the costs

Those involved with R&D are often quick to point out that the function is not one that can be carried out on a shoe-strong budget. It is normally a long-term investment, which if reduced drastically without warning, may result in lost benefits. Indeed, for results to be achieved it is likely that a 'minimum establishment' will be essential.

Even the smallest establishment on 'a man and a boy basis' would cost around £20,000/25,000 per annum, with little or nothing to show for it in the short term. This cost figure can be used as a guide to cover the employment of a graduate experienced in research, when the indirect expenses of a laboratory are considered as well as support services necessary from other departments. Accordingly, the figure selected, e.g. £20,000 may be multiplied by the number of research workers to give a rough and ready guide to the cost of the function. This figure does not include major items of expenditure on materials and equipment, but takes into account floor space likely to be occupied.

In dealing with R&D expenditure and revenue, an attempt has to be made to divide the amounts into distinct groups:

1   Specific prospects.
2   Basic research.
3   General work.
4   Customers' assignments (jobbing work).

The allocation and apportionment of costs (and sometimes revenues) is one of the most difficult areas of accounting and therefore it would be wrong to suppose that the process is relatively simple.

There might be a strong case for showing separately those costs of a
research nature and those incurred for developing actual projects.
On the other hand, development costs are for a tangible project and
often there is no doubt as to their allocation or apportionment. Once
the initial division is made, a further analysis can be developed
showing the research expenditure broken down into basic and applied;
the latter might be charged against revenue with reasonably certainty.
Where there is a problem is because the expenditure on R&D may
cover a considerably period before any tangible benefits are received.
This raises a difficulty in not knowing which part of the expenditure
incurred each year should be charged in the annual accounts. The
basic approach can be seen by reference to Figure 1.1.

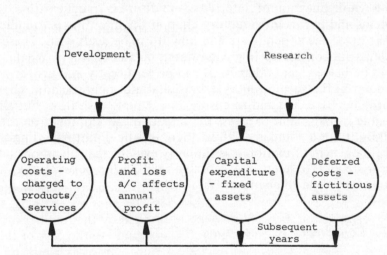

Figure 1.1   R&D: the basic classification of expenditure

1.5.3   Conventions of accounting

The 'matching' rule is now well established in accounting. It means
that the costs incurred in a particular period should be matched, as
far as possible, with the revenues that arise from incurring them. For
example, it may be decided that the research cost incurred for a
particular project will produce revenues with reasonable certainty
over the next three years. Accordingly, the research cost should be

charged against those three years, in relation to the amounts to be received. If the anticipated revenue is £10,000, £20,000 and £30,000 in years one, two and three, respectively, then the cost would be written off in the proportions of 1/6th, 2/6ths and 3/6th. However, as will be appreciated, this example is an oversimplification and begs the question on what are the current values of the cash flows.

In theory this approach should be adopted. Regrettably, in practice, there is no way of knowing with certainty how much revenue will be received nor the specific years when it will accrue. Accordingly, estimating the profitability of projects should receive careful attention. Where a profit cannot be determined because of the nature of a project – there is difficulty in separating a single project from others – then *contribution accounting* may have to be employed. This means deducting from the estimated share of sales revenue, those marginal costs attributable to the project, thus arriving at a 'contribution.'

The whole question of deferred exepnditure is fraught with problems and in this introductory chapter the intention is to indicate the nature of the expenditure and how it can be dealt with. These problems are considered in greater detail in later chapters. What should be made clear is that R&D can be very costly and proper treatment in the accounting system is vital; not only to show what the projects have cost and to ensure an adequate cash flow, but also to enable management to assess the impact of development on the profitability of a company. Whilst there is little doubt regarding the need for this vital function it is similarly evident that planning and control are vital to keep an acceptable relationship between the amount spent and the benefits obtained.

1.5.4   Consistency in accounting

Another accounting convention or principle to be observed is that of 'consistency'. Once a suitable method of accounting is determined, it should not be varied without good reason. If, because of changes in circumstances the basis of accounting is changed then this fact should be reported in the profit and loss accounts and the figures adjusted to allow for the change, when making comparisons with previous accounting periods.

1.5.5   Management accounting and budgetary control

In its most basic form, accounting for R&D means that expenditure is incurred as and when required and charged to the profit and loss account during the financial year. No attempt is made to cost individual projects, neither is there any matching of costs or revenues. Provided the company continues to earn a profit, everyone is satisfied and the results are not evaluated in financial terms.

This simple approach may satisfy some companies, but in today's competitive situation these are, likely to be in the minority. In most companies, if the function is to be of maximum value it should be integrated with the overall corporate objectives. There can be no justification for having one set of objectives for a company as a whole and another for the R&D activity; the latter should be planned and not be the result of haphazard development by the manager responsible.

This planning can take the form of simple budgets showing how much is approved for individual projects and for R&D as a whole, within each accounting period. Within this system of budgetary control, there can also be guidelines issued on the authority required to start a new project and to incur expenditure on new or existing projects. As shown in later chapters, this approach is desirable and is recommended for any company wishing to have firm management of its R&D activities.

A further desirable development of planning and control would be the design and issue of reports and statements to the board of directors and to various levels of management. These could cover corporate objectives for R&D, total expenditure, costs of individual projects and various progress reports on research activities. There could also be periodic reappraisals of projects and decisions on whether to abandon these that are not fulfilling expectations, or to introduce modifications as necessary to meet changed circumstances.

A comprehensive management accounting system can provide some of the information necessary for developing and evaluating the R&D corporate objectives and strategy. For this reason it is hoped that the principles and practice outlined in the later chapters will be considered by those who wish to operate the R&D function in an effective manner.

1.6 METHOD OF APPROACH

The intention is to look at R&D as a corporate activity, and to consider the organisation needed if the objectives are to be realised. This is then followed by an examination of what is covered in planning the R&D programme, including the principles of budgetary control.

Attention is paid to the need for control, and although these techniques are not always needed, an outline description is given of such project control techniques as PERT (Programme Evaluation and Review Technique) and CPM (Critical Path Method). In addition, the expense control of projects and the evaluation of the effectiveness of R&D is also covered.

If R&D expenditure is to be treated in a manner that gives a true reflection of the activities of a business, there should be an understanding of the nature of the costs incurred. Accordingly, an examination is made of how the expenditure can be classified and how the costs are likely to behave. This is followed by the treatment of cost involved within the annual accounts.

From an auditing point of view great care is required to ensure that the accounting treatment does expressly show a true and fair view of the R&D expenditure. As a general rule it should be stated that all revenue expenditure should be charged within the year it is incurred. Therefore only in *exceptional* and *justifiable* circumstances should R&D revenue expenditure be capitalised and carried forward into subsequent years. Moreover, when this is done, there should be a satisfactory treatment in the writing off of expenditure year-by-year. The practice of making annual charges that fluctuate according to the profit earned is unlikely to give a realistic assessment of results.

A vital area in company management is to ensure an adequate cash flow. As far as R&D is concerned, this means that where the expenditure is not written off each year, a close watch must be maintained on how much is being spent. A company may appear to be earning a considerable profit which could lull management and the public into thinking that there are no problems, but where R&D expenditure is carried forward into future years, there must be sufficient cash available to meet all commitments. A company should not be allowed to get into the situation where it is earning large profits, but is unable to meet its debts!

If the procedures are to be fully understood, written instructions should be provided in the form of an R&D manual. As a preliminary to this requirement, attention should be drawn to the need to design a suitable system that covers the necessary requirements for initiating, evaluating, and controlling the functions in its various phases. The design of systems and the related accounting procedures are covered in the latter part of this book. There is no one ready-made system for any company, but it is hoped that the principles outlined will at least indicate the major requirements.

ED14 (Exposure Draft 14) proposes that expenditure incurred be written in the year of expenditure, but the cost of fixed assets relating to R&D should be capitalised and written off over their useful life. This suggestion is logical, but means that considerable sums can be carried forward into future periods! Because costs are incurred on fixed assets this does not guarantee that the R&D will

be successful. In many cases this 'rule' may result in expenditure
being carried forward that would have been better written off
when incurred.

2
THE COMPASS OF CORPORATE R&D ACTIVITY

As indicated in Chapter 1, there is difficulty in stating where the corporate R&D function ends and where other functions take over. Typical questions that have to be resolved are:

1   Is market research an R&D or a sales function?
2   Should the design and implementation of improvements in service industries be classified as an R&D activity?

This chapter attempts to provide some guidance on these and related questions of definition and classification.

Throughout industry, companies concerned with R&D, if properly organised, operate with clearly defined objectives, and have an appropriately staffed and organised department to pursue them. But no two R&D departments will carry out precisely the same function – the phrase 'research and development' will have been defined differently in each case in order to meet the organisational and accounting needs of each company. 'Basic' research to one company may be 'applied' research to another. A standard definition and classification of R&D activity could only be achieved by unacceptable over-simplification.

Three broad categories of R&D activity are referred to in this book,
and defined as follows:

1   *Basic research*   Work directed towards improving understand-
    ing in a particular field without regard to its specific use. The
    probability of success in basic research cannot be predicted with
    certainty.
2   *Applied research*   The preliminary exploration of a concept
    with a view to some known or presumed useful application.
    Applied research is normally based on principles established by
    basic research.
3   *Development work* which may also incorporate the *design* func-
    tion. This final stage covers the commercial exploitation of the
    results of the research effort. The need for *cost-effectiveness*
    is a predominant consideration in development work.

   The three categories are characterised by the following key questions:

1   *Basic research*   What further knowledge is desirable (in a
    particular field of interest)?
2   *Applied research*   Is the hoped-for development technically
    feasible, is there a likely profitable market, and can the company
    finance the work?
3   *Development work*   Can the product or process be successfully
    converted into a financially viable proposition, and how is this
    to be achieved?

2.1.1   Basic research

Most investment in basic research is at substantial risk. Expensive
equipment and highly paid staff may be employed for prolonged
periods without tangible results. Even if the research succeeds, the
successful development of the new product or process may only
be achieved by investing considerable further capital at a high risk.
   Basic research is mainly carried out by government departments
and universities, which means that much of the search for knowledge
that may benefit society at large is financed reasonably enough from
public money. However, many far-sighted and wealthy industrial
companies carry out basic research. Corporate basic research activity,
whilst preserving the characteristic of seeking knowledge without
regard to the specific eventual use to which knowledge may be put,
is usually concentrated in those technological areas where any

discovery would have a fair chance of adoption in the furtherance of corporate long-term objectives.

2.1.2 *Applied research*

Applied research represents the take-off point in the launching of promising concepts towards practical fruition and as such usually represents a less daunting investment prospect than basic research. Fortunately, most corporate research activity falls within the applied research category.

Applied research can be regarded as the focal point of two distinct branches of basic research (see Figure 2.1). These are:

1   The knowledge of basic social needs or new broad areas of commercial opportunity.
2   New products or processes at the conceptual stage.

Successful applied research is the finding of a much needed product,

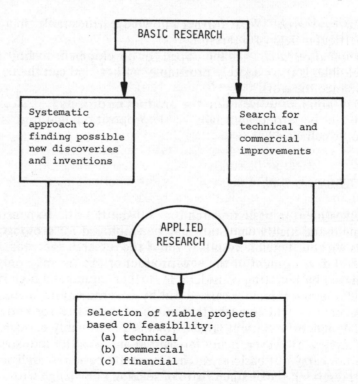

Figure 2.1 Applied research - focal point of the two branches of basic research

process or method, followed by a technical feasibility study of the
intended application of basic knowledge. Liason with the production
department should be established at the stage when technical feasibility is being considered. Good communication between production
and R&D can prevent time from being spent on impractical ideas.
There should also be a close link with the marketing possibilities and
a watch kept on the technological developments.

2.1.3 Development work

Corporate development work usually carries the prospect of return
on money invested in the foreseeable future, and when compared with
applied research, is more predictable, and therefore tends to be easier
to budget, and more readily financed. Many companies that carry out
development work conduct neither basic nor applied research.

Multi-disciplinary teams are often used in work of this nature.
Consider, for example, the teamwork required for the successful
development of a new product:

1   The R&D department contributes the technical understanding
     of the item under development.
2   The marketing department must form a balanced view as to the
     commercial success of the new product, and determine how it
     is to be presented to customers. Market 'know-how' may result
     in product modifications to improve customer appeal.
3   The design department must strike a balance between conflicting
     requirements such as the best use of materials, strength, cheap-
     ness, ease of manufacture, durability and the aesthetic require-
     ments. Effective liaison between the design and production
     functions is vital in mass-production functions and in those pro-
     ducing heavy equipment or machines to customers' specifications.
4   The chief development executive must control these activities,
     balancing development time and expense against potential im-
     provement of the product. He must also consider the budgeted
     activity or production capacity, an important factor in capital
     intensive industries.
5   The accountant can advise on the availability of finance and
     the likely effect on cash flow, as well as providing comparative
     costs for different alternatives.

2.2   AREAS OF CORPORATE R&D ACTIVITY

The best known areas that may be covered within corporate R&D

activity are summarised in Figure 2.2. It will be seen that the function extends well beyond the invention and development of products and processes. The 'Organisation Studies' may not be constructed as R&D in many companies — rather they will be treated as management services. However, the important requirement is that no function should operate in isolation from others. Market research is included as an R&D activity, but should not necessarily be controlled by the chief R&D executive, as it is advisable to make this function the responsibility of a marketing executive. This is an arbitrary arrangement as illustrated by the close liaison required between the market research and R&D departments when the replacement of an existing product with a new one is under consideration. The departments must work closely together in comparing the merits and demerits of the existing and the new products, and evaluating any problems which change could bring, in order that the correct decision may be taken when or if the existing product should be phased out and the new one introduced. When the study of new and improved services is classified as R&D, the same principles and procedures as for product studies should apply.

2.3   A PRACTICAL ILLUSTRATION

The following simplified case study illustrates how the results of basic research were applied in the improvement of a particular metal extraction process, in which impure powdered metal alloy is roasted in a controlled atmosphere, in order to oxidise one metal but not others, so that the oxidised metal can later be separated by acid leaching. Traditional roasting furnaces were unsatisfactory as the temperature varied from point to point inside the furnace, with the result that the roasted material was not of consistent chemical composition. In this illustration, the basic research was not conducted by the company that researched and developed the process improvement.

2.3.1   Basic research

A study was made of the behaviour of beds of small particles subjected to fluidisation by means of the upwards passage of air under pressure. The object of this research was to establish a mathematical basis describing the inter-relationship of variable factors, such as the range of particle sizes, air pressure, temperature, and degree of fluidisation.

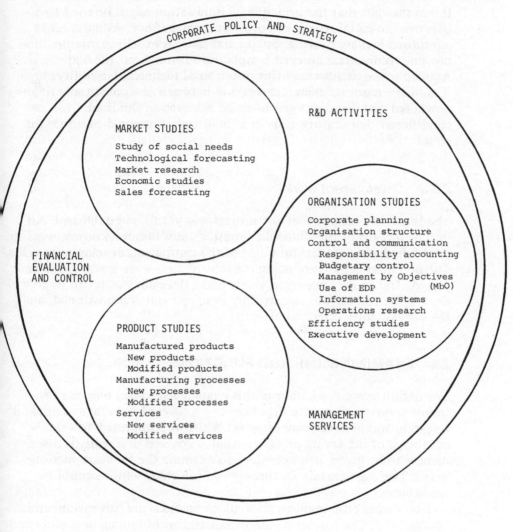

CORPORATE POLICY AND STRATEGY

R&D ACTIVITIES

MARKET STUDIES

Study of social needs
Technological forecasting
Market research
Economic studies
Sales forecasting

ORGANISATION STUDIES

Corporate planning
Organisation structure
Control and communication
 Responsibility accounting
 Budgetary control
 Management by Objectives
 Use of EDP   (MbO)
 Information systems
 Operations research
Efficiency studies
Executive development

FINANCIAL
EVALUATION
AND CONTROL

PRODUCT STUDIES

Manufactured products
 New products
 Modified products
Manufacturing processes
 New processes
 Modified processes
Services
 New services
 Modified services

MANAGEMENT
SERVICES

Figure 2.2 Possible areas of R&D activity

It was thought that the principle of fluidisation might be used to improve the metal roasting process described above. As particles in a fluidised bed are moving rapidly and there is excellent mixing, it is possible to maintain an even temperature throughout the bed. Applied research answered this question of technical feasibility: 'Could the required chemical reaction between one constituent of the powdered metal and oxygen in air be achieved in fluidised conditions?' Laboratory tests in a small-scale furnace showed that it could.

2.3.3   *Development work*

The financial feasibility of the project was yet to be established. An outline design for the 'fluosolids roaster', as it became known, was established and an estimate made of the capital and development costs. The potential benefits of using the new process were investigated and costed. The project appeared viable and a decision was taken to go ahead. The roaster was successfully designed and commissioned, and has subsequently operated effectively.

2.4   EXAMINING THE R&D FUNCTIONS

The definitions given earlier in this chapter have been reduced to simple terms to show what is likely to be covered in basic and applied research, and in development work. Whilst this approach has the advantage of indicating precisely what is covered, if a realistic assessment is to be made, it is necessary to examine the function in more detail. There are certain features present in R&D which should be made clear.

Two words prominent in all writings on R&D are 'invention' and 'innovation'. The former means originating or obtaining new ideas and then developing them to the point where they have a practical and commercial application. Innovation is sometimes used with the same meaning, but it is generally taken to mean the commercial exploitation of the invention, so that it can be produced and sold in sufficient quantity to earn an acceptable profit.

Not all R&D directors and managers agree with the orthodox definitions given earlier. Some suggest that the tendency to look upon applied research as a lower type of work than basic research, especially

when linked with technology, may discourage the personnel concerned.
However, whether theoretical research has a useful purpose is also
arguable, because arguments can be advanced against employing top
class scientists in the pursuit of knowledge for its own sake. With
applied research, irrespective of the commercial motive, there is the
possibility that the new inventions will in the long term, benefit mankind.

This idea that some types of research are 'better' than others, sometimes raises the question whether R&D should be subjected to
controls from managers and accountants. It can be argued that if a
company is to give its research workers the fullest possible assistance
and scope, then there should be no artificial barrier against progress.
It should be acknowledged that control − the comparison of actual
with planned results and subsequent corrective action − cannot be
applied in the same degree as with say standardised production. But,
a company tends to have limited resources, and for this reason it
must be impressed upon research personnel that the spending of shareholders' money must be justified; any investment should have a
reasonable chance of paying for itself within the foreseeable future.

A useful breakdown of R&D into categories, places, people,
processes and outcome is given in Table 2.1. This tabulation shows
the breakdown of the different types of research and introduces two
new terms:

1   *Fundamental research* is concerned with the investigation into
    nature and the physical world. As indicated earlier, this type of
    research is carried out at universities, in government departments,
    and at research associations, the latter often backed by govern-
    ment departments or by industries. In practice, the fundamental
    research may impinge upon the basic research carried out in
    industry so that both types of research can be carried out in the
    same establishments, so this distinction between fundamental
    and basic may not always be clear.
2   *Technical support* is primarily concerned with providing a wider
    range of technical services to customers, including dealing with
    their queries in the form of requests for a wider application of
    the product, or because of troubles arising from its use. Products
    under this heading might cover all functional areas − manufactur-
    ing, marketing, technical development, and others. Often the
    projects are of short duration, extending over periods range from
    a few days to a few months. In some cases with a major customer,
    there may be a continuous assignment. Technical services may
    also extend into the area of quality improvement, or maintaining
    existing quality. In industries where maintenance of high quality
    products is essential, such as pharmaceuticals or aircraft com-

TABLE 2.1 Matrix for universal definition of research and development

CATEGORY	PEOPLE	PLACE	PURPOSE	PROCESS	OUTCOME
I Fundamental research Pure research, academic research	Creative, inquisitive, motivated by scientific tradition	Universities, non-profit foundations, Government laboratories, research associations	Seeking better understanding of the unknown, no specific orientation	Investigating new phenomena, discovering secrets of nature, verifying theories of physical world	Research papers presented to, and evaluated by, scientific peers
II Basic research Long-range research	Creative, inquisitive, wider discipline group than for fundamental research	Universities in liason with industry, Government laboratories, non-profit foundations, research associations, industry	Orientated long-range research on materials, components, performance, relationships of products, etc., support for development	Investigating new phenomena, creating or discovering new processes, components, devices, materials	Hypotheses on materials, processes, products, components, performance characteristics under varying conditions, testing of hypotheses
III Applied research Invention, technological	Creative, inquisitive, a wider discipline group than for basic research	Industrial, university and commercial laboratories, research associations	Exploration of new product and process creation, satisfying requirements as yet unsatisfied	Testing basic research hypotheses modifying existing materials, processes and products by substitution or recombination	Hypotheses or knowledge of natural synthetic materials, processes, tests of uncertainties, proof of technical feasibility
IV Development New products, processes, improvements, new applications, evolutionary	Multidiscipline teams of scientists, engineers, social scientists, aided by marketing, production and finance	Industrial laboratories and pilot plants	Creation of satisfactory new product or process	Resolving major technological aspects of new products or processes	Technical specifications and production and marketing requirements for new products or processes
V Technical support Application engineering, cost reduction, product engineering, customer technologies, quality control	Engineers, scientists and technicians	Industrial laboratories and production facilities or customer locations	Giving supplier and especially customer satisfaction to maintain market position; design work indirectly affected	Employing qualified scientists and engineers with substantial resources to match varying requirements of commercialisation of R&D	Technical services, trouble-shooting, applications, engineering, reports

ponents, there should be a constant watch on the possibilities of
deviating form minimum standards. In some companies it may be
advisable to concentrate part of R&D effort on quality improvement.

2.5   DEVELOPING A PATTERN FOR R&D PROJECTS

There is no standard procedure for developing and improving new
products and methods, but the following stages are generally found
necessary with a project. The following pattern is typical although
not applicable in all situations:

1   Establish that a problem exists and ascertain whether this is
    similar to any that have arisen previously.
2   Decide if the problem is solvable, and if so, what are the best
    methods of approach.
3   Select the most appropriate method of approach, and obtain
    suitable equipment and other requirements.
4   Carry out experiments or other necessary work, so that infor-
    mation is available for the possible solution.
5   Carry out an economic feasibility study to find out whether
    the new product or method is likely to be a commercial success.
6   Examine the technical problems of production and marketing.
7   Prepare prototypes and where appropriate, build a pilot plant.
8   Once the production and marketing problems have been solved,
    commence production, selling and distribution on a commercial
    scale.

The order in which these stages will be taken will depend upon the
problems and the type of business concerned. Throughout, attention
will be paid to the technical problems, both in marketing and production, as well as the financial justification for the work to be done.
    In many cases, the R&D costs may be quite small up to the point
where full-scale commercial production is sanctioned, but after this
stage, failure can lead to considerable expense. At worst, it can mean
the withdrawal of a product from the market; in other cases it can
mean calling in a product for modification or adjustment − this occurs
from time to time in the motor car industry when defects are found
after a new model has been put on sale. It has also occurred with
drugs and cigarettes.
    From an accounting point-of-view, financial planning should cover
all the essential stages. Work up to the point of commercial production
would be covered in the R&D budgets. Beyond that point, there
must be justification for the new plant and equipment required, but

this justification should not be left until the final stages have been reached, because there may be no funds available for carrying out the work. When a project has reached a point where success is reasonably certain, attention should be paid to two important aspects:

1   Confirmation that the investment in R&D can be justified. (this would have been assessed earlier).
2   Financing the investment from existing resources or by raising new funds.

A common mistake is to ignore the problems of financing until it is too late to obtain the necessary capital. Alternatively, the company that appears to have a potential winner on its books, suddenly finds it is not able to proceed further because there is difficulty in quantifying the likely outcome of investing the necessary funds.

If finance is not available at the correct time a company may have to abandon the project or sell the results to another company, or it may decide to go ahead with limited resources in the hope that the cash flow from the sales of the new invention will help to finance further expansion. With some companies this approach might succeed, but often there are delays caused by technical marketing problems which cannot always be anticipated.

Unless the company has reasonable financial backing to cover this difficult period, serious liquidity problems may jeopardise its future.

2.6   FINANCING R&D

For major projects, it may be necessary to obtain finance by raising new equity capital in the open market, or from existing shareholders, or loans may be obtained by the issue of debentures. This is done on the assumption that the increased earnings will more than offset the payments in dividends and interest to those who supply the capital or loans.

In the interests of financial prudence, any substantial increase in share capital or loans should be backed by evidence of likely success. Accordingly, it is likely that *development* work is done more likely to be able to show adequate justification of the proposal made. At the other extreme, basic research may be so hazardous that there would be great difficulty in forecasting the outcome.

R&D should be a continuous process and therefore an attempt should be made to cover a substantial part of the cost from current earnings. As will be shown later, there are differences of approach to the question whether the expenditure should be written off in one year, or be deferred for apportioning over the years in which benefits

from the research are expected to accrue. Leaving aside the question
of dealing with expenditure on a year-to-year basis, it is still
necessary to consider how additional costs are to be financed.

Companies that are constantly striving to improve should be
regarded as high risk in their operations, but if they are successful,
profits can be high. If R&D is not effective and no new products
are made, there may be no profit at all.

With successful products the prices charged should include a
substantial margin to cover both past R&D activity and that required
in the future.

For many companies there is no guarantee that all projects will
produce tangible results; failure is a common feature within the R&D
function even where projects have reached the advanced stage of new
product launch. Market research may indicate a considerable demand
for a product, judging from experience in other countries and possibly
in sample areas in the UK but unfortunately, there is no guarantee
of success, and many failures can be quoted. Condensed soups, various
kinds of alcoholic drinks and even motor cars have all failed miserably,
even though the earlier signs indicated considerable success.

New products developed by companies may, to some extent, be
protected by patents and trade marks and, of course the store of
knowledge and expertise that is available from the R&D function.
During the period when this protection operates, prices can be fairly
high and the profit margin considerable. Technology is in a constant
state of development, and competition comes from substitute products, or from new or improved products which derive from inventions that have already been developed. This may mean that prices can
fall significantly, within a short period. The classicial case was the
development of the ball-point pen, but it has also occurred in
integrated miniaturised circuitry, silicones, nylon, and cortisones. A
company will wish to maintain prices as high as possible or sell a
large volume of output, and thus be able to cover the costs of R&D as
well as the normal costs of producing and marketing.

2.7 THE SIZE OF THE BUSINESS

In the USA about 85 per cent of industrial R&D is undertaken by
companies employing more than 5000 people. In Britain, 93 per cent
of industrial R&D is carried out by companies employing more than
2000, and only 1 per cent by those employing less than 300. However,
it should be appreciated that a considerable volume of R&D is carried
out within small firms by the owner or other key personnel and often
is not classified as such or even recorded in any special way. The cost
may therefore appear under various headings including 'Production'

28 or 'Administration'. Nonetheless, it is of significant importance and
should not be dismissed lightly.

These statistics suggest a clear correlation between the extent of a
company's R&D effort and the size of the company itself. This
relationship is to be expected, as a vigorous policy of developing new
profitable products will, under normal circumstances, lead to inevitable growth in profits, capital employed and numbers employed. This
tendency will be accentuated, as the statistics imply, once the
company has reached a threshold size where economics of scale begin
to apply, and where corporate size and status permit access to external
sources of capital not normally available to the smaller company.

2.8   BENEFITS OF R&D

The methods of evaluating the benefits from R&D are covered in
subsequent chapters. In this section of the book, a *general* outline is
given to show some of the reasons why firms may devote substantial
resources to R&D.

2.8.1   Economies of scale

Economies of scale, of whatever type, will often produce savings in
the consumption of resources, and should assist the promotion of
further growth. It is contended that a major reason for the recent high
level of acquisitive growth by British and American companies, has
been the attraction of savings from spreading the high cost of marketing
and R&D expertise over larger volumes of output.

Such economies in R&D are seen where major companies in a
particular industry cooperate to finance a common research establishment for the benefit of all participants. Examples are the Motor
Industry Research Association and the Tobacco Research Council,
which provide test facilities for members, and research into technical
problems of common interest to the industry.

2.8.2   A summary of some of the reasons

1   There is evidence that companies which invest in R&D can grow
      substantially [see, for example, *The Charpie Report* (1967) which
      gives the growth rates for such companies as Texas Instruments,
      Xerox, IBM and 3M, over the period 1945-1965]. Although not
      all companies are successful in producing new products and
      methods which lead to substantial growth, for those that make

the right decisions the benefits can be enormous.

2   New products may be essential to counteract competition. There is considerable evidence to show that this factor influences such companies as soap and detergent manufacturers, razor blade manufacturers (Wilkinson Sword and Gillette) and those producing cosmetics.

3   There is a hope that substantial cost savings will be achieved. Companies such as ICI Limited and The International Synthetic Rubber Company Limited are examples where new processes have provided considerable savings. The *value analysis approach*, where products and methods are examined critically, has resulted in considerable cost reductions for many products.

4   Large profit margins are expected, especially when the product is in its first year.

5   It is necessary to keep abreast of technological developments in production processes. In many process industries new developments have resulted in the development of fully automated plants. This has occurred in chemical manufacturing, flour milling, and similar industries. Often this process results from the combined initiative of the equipment manufacturer and the users of that equipment, but this is not necessarily the case.

2.8.3   Size and ability to finance R&D

Company size and stability can also dictate the extent of ability to finance R&D. The large company may have a material advantage over its smaller competitor if, in the knowledge that it can afford to channel most of its *internally* generated finance to the research and development of a product, it can subsequently expect to obtain the necessary finance for full-scale manufacturing and marketing facilities from *external* sources, such as the capital market or central government agencies.

2.8.4   Size and organisation

Although R&D tends to be carried out by the larger companies, this does not mean that relatively small businesses do not achieve significant success. Indeed, innovation can benefit from an informal structure and the presence of an 'entrepreneur type' manager, who is willing and able to follow ideas through to their completion. As will be appreciated, with growth in size, companies become more difficult to manage and procedures for planning and controlling become more complex. One result of a formal organisational structure may be to lengthen the time between the initiation of an idea and its successful development and to discourage that commitment which researchers might otherwise derive from a more *laissez faire* environment. The R&D function, to be successful, need not necessarily be on a large scale, especially if linked in with results obtained from universities, laboratories and other government establishments. Statistics produced from research carried out in the USA have shown that major producers tend to account for a considerable number of significant American developments. However, the greater number, more than two thirds, come from small companies and independent inventors.

The lesson to be learnt it seems, is that for successful innovation, finance alone is not enough. There need to be staff who have the appropriate ideas and who can develop these in a manner which results in tangible benefits. Innovation is often produced from the efforts of a few, rather than from masses, of resources. Nevertheless, it must be stressed that many R&D projects require the backing of large companies, to be able to finance the work on the scale required for success. It may be that in many industries a relatively small improvement can bring about the possibilities of considerable gain; on the other hand, when attempting to improve a large scale production methods, where much effort has already been undertaken, the probability of a large payoff may be slim.

3
R&D
ORGANISATION

A detailed study of organisational theory applied to R&D is outside the scope of this book, but, it is hoped that, by concentrating on basic principles and generalising as much as is practicable, the reader will achieve a better understanding of the R&D environment in which he works and with which he is familiar.

3.1   INTRODUCTION TO ORGANISATION

3.1.1   What does organisation cover?

The company organisation chart (see Figure 3.1) is a useful management tool that is familiar to most people. Interconnected boxes are used to portray formal relationships in the organisation, each box representing a job function. However, too frequently, executives tend to consider that their responsibility for developing and structuring their organisation ends with the production of an organisation chart; company organisation is a complex subject which requires more attention than this.

The word 'organisation' has been defined in many different ways.

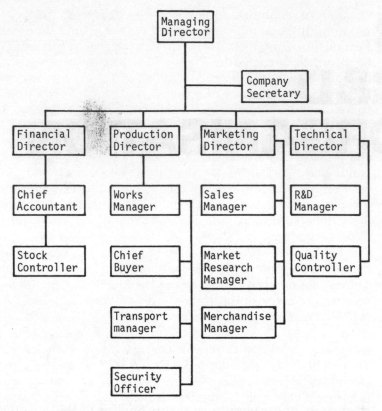

Figure 3.1 Typical manufacturing company organisation chart

Some writers on the subject consider only structural aspects, whilst others concentrate on the behavioural side of business. A broad view is taken in this book, where organisation is looked upon as the manner in which a company deploys its available resources, including funds, in order to achieve its objectives. This liberal interpretation is reflected in the following summary of what organization covers.

1   *Authority structure*   The formal arrangement of job functions which serves as the foundation for business activity. A company's authority structure determines:
   a   who reports to whom;
   b   the management strata through which responsibility is to be delegated;
   c   the main working groups in the company, probably to be known as departments;
   d   the basis for establishing accountability.
2   *Communication structure*   The formal information network linking job functions throughout the company. The main

channels of communication will run parallel to authority *33*
relationships, communication taking place in both directions.
Formal 'horizontal' channels will exist so that departments may
be informed of each others' activities. 'Vertical' channels which
do not follow authority relationships will also exist: for example,
the production director of a subsidiary company; who reports
to his chief executive, may be required to keep the *group* chief
executive directly informed as to specific performance indicators.

3   *Arrangement of work-flows*   The inter-relationship of systems
and processes by which the company's business operations are
conducted. Work-flows frequently cross departmental boundaries;
for example, in an integrated company, product development will
include work passing through the R&D, production, and sales
departments; the accounts department will also be`concerned at a
number of stages.

4   *The employment of people*   An organisation, in the last analysis,
comprises a group of people working towards a common goal.
The employment of people of the right calibre is one of the highest
priorities of an organisation wishing to achieve success.

5   *Informal relationships*   The basis for organisation is the position-
ing of people in a formal structure. Informal relationships, however,
will always exist and cannot be ignored in any study of organisation.
There will always be a 'grapevine', just as there will be particular
groupings of people at coffee and lunch breaks. The right kind of
informal relationships should be encouraged by management as
these are essential to the smooth running of any organisation.

6   *The employment of technology*   A properly organised company
can operate effectively without the aid of sophisticated management tools and techniques. But in a competitive and increasingly
complex world the use of advanced, and often expensive technology, becomes increasingly necessary. Today, in all but the smallest organisations, business activity can benefit from the case of
modern tools for decision-making, methods of data processing,
control techniques and means of communication.

The above ideas are incorporated in the schematic representation
of organisation given in Figure 3.2.The main elements of organisation
may be further illustrated by reference to a typical organisational problem. Assume that a company operating division is achieving poor
profit results which are largely due to the individual chief executive
not anticipating certain difficulties and opportunities. The problem
may be examined in different ways, possibilities being as follows:

1   *A structural solution*   The division could be badly structured
internally, or its relationships with the centre or with fellow

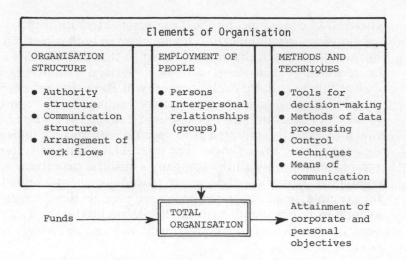

Figure 3.2 The elements and role of organisation

operating divisions could be wrong. Authority structure might require changing, or perhaps better communications would solve the problem. The exact solution will depend upon the detailed circumstances of the case. As an example, the divisional chief executive might be spending too much time in discussing the day-to-day running of the division with subordinates, in which case his span of control is perhaps too wide — a problem that could be solved by adjustment to the authority structure.

2   *A 'people' solution*   The division might employ men of inadequate calibre, or there may be personality clashes, and morale could be low. In the example, the divisional chief executive may not be up to the job, in which case the solution might be to fire him, or, he may have qualities which could be better employed elsewhere in the organisation. His failure to anticipate events may have been rooted in poor personal relations with key men in his organisation. Better informal contacts with his colleagues might have improved his 'feel' for the business.

3   *A technical solution*   The division may be backward in its use of management tools and techniques. The divisional chief executive may be floundering owing to a lack of properly analysed information on the division's past performance and that of competitors; the installation of appropriate costing and budgetary control and planning systems might help.

Every organisation, is complex — covering structure, people and technology — and many variables must be considered. A smoothly

functioning organisation depends upon a correct inter-relationship
between variables; the system is dynamic: a change in one variable will
result in, or require change in another.

3.1.2   How is organisation determined?

Any formal structure will have advantages and disadvantages. Management's aim must be to develop the formal structure that appears most
advantageous then to offset its disadvantages by means of good
communications and successful informal relationships.

The short answer, therefore, to the question 'How is organisation
determined?' is − It depends! Whatever the commercial environment
in which a company trades, it must organise according to its objectives.
A company's objectives will determine, in turn:

1   What work requires to be done.
2   What job functions should exist in view of this work.
3   What organisation should exist in view of these job functions.

Whilst it is inadvisable to be too specific as to the determinants of
good and bad organisation, the following are some of the fundamental
principles of good organisation that can be identified.

a   Funds should be allocated so as to provide a combination of
      people, plant, and equipment of sufficient size and capability to
      handle the work requirements dictated by corporate objectives.
b   Organisational arrangements should enable the running of the
      business to be decentralised where appropriate and necessary,
      whilst the important function of policy direction remains within
      the board. This includes the setting up of a formal structure which
      facilitates effective delegation of authority and responsibility.
      Each employee in the organisation should be made aware of the
      responsibilities for which he will be held accountable.
c   A 'feed-back' mechanism should exist, so that the operation of the
      organisation can be monitored, coordinated and controlled. The
      mechanism used should be appropriate to the nature of the work.
d   The right people must be recruited in relation to the work to be
      done, and there should be harmony of personal interests and
      organisational goals.
e   The organisation must not be regarded as inflexible.

The application of these principles will vary from company to company.
As will be seen later, a certain amount of adaptation is required when
the principles are applied in an R&D context.

Section 3.1 dealt with organisation problems in general terms. In this section the nature of the R&D function is considered and some of the conflicting interests that can arise when organising are examined. Not all companies need to pursue R&D activity but, in the vast majority of cases, corporate objectives will determine that technological advances must be made to ensure long-term profitability. The job to be done, is thus determined, primarily, by the discovery and development of new products and processes. The next step is to examine the nature of R&D work before considering appropriate arrangements of the organisational variables.

3.2.1   The nature of R&D work

The work is complex and it is an area about which it is not easy to generalise; but three characteristics are predominant:
1   *Creative*   If R&D is to provide new and improved products and processes, the corresponding work must, by definition, be creative. Basic research is directed towards the acquisition of new knowledge; applied research and development work towards the creation of new technology in one form or another.
2   *Unprogrammed*   Even though a generalised approach to the planning of problems is successfully established, it is difficult to set a specific approach to a particular problem requiring original thought. This is because R&D is by its nature unpredictable and depends largely for its outcome upon an intuitive approach less frequently observed in other functions. Development work may be planned and controlled and technical specifications set, with a deadline to meet, but even this activity is not programmed in the true sense. In development work, problems requiring original thought for their solution will inevitably arise. Basic research, because it deals with the unknown cannot be programmed in any detail.
3   *Technical*   R&D work frequently demands detailed knowledge of one or more scientific disciplines, and may be highly specialised. Usually, therefore, the personnel must be qualified and trained in a technical field usually to a high level.

3.2.2   Organising for R&D

With R&D, certain principles of good organisation come into conflict with organisational requirements dictated by the nature of the work, so it may be necessary to adopt a compromise approach.

The main difficulties are as follows:

1 *Conflicts with organisation principles*   The creative nature of
the work demands that ideas should have freedom of development in
the broad areas determined by the R&D objectives. This conflicts to
some extent with the second and third principles of organisation (that
tasks should be directed, coordinated and controlled) and is in direct
opposition to the concept of a rigid authoritarian organisation
structure. How can innovation and change be expected to flourish if
R&D activity is smothered by layer upon layer of bureaucracy?

The setting up of a research department independent of other corporate functions would seem one obvious solution. Thinking and
planning would be separated from the day-to-day running of the
business. This solution, although adopted by some companies, will
be seen later to have disadvantages which sometimes render it unacceptable.

2 *Job descriptions may restrict initiative*   Developing job descriptions is a feature of sound organisation that may conflict with
the need for a creative environment in which unprogrammed activity
may be successfully conducted. If the areas of responsibility are
defined precisely and in detail, will this limit the activities covered?
Yet having a job description is desirable in one sense because it
enables work to be related with some certainty to corporate objectives. However a precise job description is inconsistent with role
flexibility, which is essential for dealing with R&D jobs that crop up
at short notice, and for the smooth running of any organisation using
the multi-disciplinary project team approach to research.

For this reason it is desirable that any description used is 'open-
ended', thus allowing the required freedom of action within the
constraints of the corporate objectives.

3 *The hierarchy may block liaison*   The technical nature of R&D
brings its own problems, chief amongst them being top management's
frequent inability to comprehend what the research staff is doing and
why. In this connection, the R&D chief executive has an important
role to play, and it is essential that his status in the organisation
should permit effective liasion with top management. The main tasks
of the R&D chief executive are discussed in Section 3.6.1.

In considering the organisation of the function the following must
be borne in mind.

a   its structure;
b   behavioural aspects;

techniques used in planning and control.

These are dealt with as follows. An analysis of authority structure is developed in Sections 3.3 and 3.4 with discussion of communications structure in Section 3.5. People and their relationships are considered in Section 3.6, and finally, the methods and techniques used in organising R&D are examined in Chapters 5 and 7, dealing respectively with planning and control of the programme.

3.3 PLACE OF R&D IN COMPANY STRUCTURE

Every board of directors of every company must decide for itself the importance of R&D. If long-term corporate objectives dictate that the function has a full and important role to play in the corporate future, as in the majority of cases they will, then the question arises of what organisation structure would best serve to integrate this activity with other corporate functions.

The possibility of segregating the activity from the rest of the business (centralised R&D) was mentioned earlier in this chapter. The idea suggested itself because of the differing natures of this activity and other business functions, mainly because an authoritarian structure is not conducive to good R&D. But there is another possibility, that of providing appropriate business cost centres with their own R&D sections (decentralised R&D). This approach may be advocated because, in a changing world, organisations must change and adapt as business circumstances change. A rigid authoritarian structure is more readily changed if there is frequent discussion of new ideas between R&D men and line executives. This is more likely when the function is based in divisions with a direct link with the divisional board and managers. However, in attempting to create the correct atmosphere care would be taken to avoid a multiplicity of research units with consequent overlap and duplication.

3.3.1 Centralised or decentralised R&D?

In deciding the place of R&D in the organisation structure the main choices open to management are:

1 Wholly centralised.
2 Wholly decentralised.
3 Centralised according to company profit or responsibility centres (operating factories or divisions).

The first two possibilities have attractions, but each suffers from a
lack of the other's advantages.

Centralised R&D has the following advantages:

1   The function is separated organisationally, possibly geographi-
cally, from the rest of the business. This means that:
    a   the R&D unit may be structured in a creative environment;
    b   R&D men are not drawn into the solving of day-to-day
problems, so that full attention may be given to work
with a medium or long-term perspective, such as basic
research.
2   The research effect is concentrated as an organisational unit,
which means that:
    a   the function may be better equipped to take on major
projects;
    b   there is maximum scope for cross-fertilisation of ideas;
    c   peaks and troughs in demand on R&D time are more
easily smoothed in a large department.
3   More effective supervision of projects and a better prospect of
setting up budgetary control with an accountant or cost clerk
to assist.

Decentralised research offers the following advantages:

1   A close relationship between R&D men and line executives,
which result in:
    a   an orientation of R&D work towards solving business
problems;
    b   a better appreciation amongst line executives of the con-
tinuing need for improvement and change in products,
processes, and business procedures.
2   Cost-centre management has access to R&D and to some extent
can control one of its most valuable resources. Absolute control
may be undesirable because coordination of R&D will be a vital
requirement.

The *third* of the *choices* listed above, that of centralisation according to company profit centres, is an attempt to create an organisation
unit that enjoys the advantages of both centralised and decentralised
R&D. Under this arrangement, administration of the function is
centralised, but planning control of the work programme rests with
the profit-centre management. The main danger with this type of
organisation is the possible development of a power struggle between the administrative heads of R&D and the profit-centre manager.
However, this danger is minimised if there is a clear understanding at

the outset that divisional management have the authority to determine *what* shall be done, and R&D to determine *how* it shall be done. A useful study of this form of organisation has been made by Reeves [1].

3.3.2   Factors affecting the organisation

The manner in which a company organises R&D will depend ultimately upon the company's objectives, but more directly upon:

1   Size.
2   Company organisation structure in particular; whether the company is decentralised.
3   The nature of the business.

A small company (turnover under £20 million) is more likely to find that a wholly centralised R&D is the most effective. This is because there appears to be a critical size below which the effectiveness of an R&D unit falls off. It is likely that teams of a reasonable number of qualified staff, e.g. 20 or more, will tend to set better results (on a per capita basis) than smaller teams. They are able to look at extensive problems and with the pooling of ideas to get better results. Small companies are ill-advised to fragment their research effort by decentralisation and may find it better served to use outside consultants rather than to operate an R&D function of their own. Only exceptionally would it be wise to locate small R&D units in a decentralised situation such as when they wish to be near the problems which arise.

Larger companies are normally able to choose any one of the three possible approaches. Most large companies have decentralised R&D departments but many others, whilst having decentralised control of the work programme, retain R&D administration centrally. Much depends upon the nature of a company's business, in particular the extent, if any, to which basic research is carried on. Basic research is best conducted in an 'academic' atmosphere as far removed as possible from day-to-day business pressures, and, an isolated basic research unit may well exist, regardless of other organisational arrangements for this function.

The following section, which deals with internal organisation of the function, is applicable equally to the organisation of *(a)* a wholly centralised R&D unit, and *(b)* each unit of a decentralised system.

A first-class salesman does not necessarily make a good sales director; the skills of selling are somewhat removed from those of administration. R&D is analagous in that the skills of a scientist are equally if not further removed from the administrator's than those of the salesman. The scientist's studious and thoroughgoing approach to his work may even breed a balance of personal qualities much different from those required for the quick and efficient handling of day-to-day problems. The logical step, therefore, is to separate technical and administrative functions from R&D.

3.4.1   Technical organisation

Research and development technical staff can be organised in different ways. A formal organisation structure is normally used, but is often modified by the superimposition of arrangements which aim to ensure that a flexible approach to complex problems can be adopted. There are several types of formal structure, each of which may be used either alone or in combination with others, but despite the predominance of certain types of formal structure it is difficult to generalise with regard to the R&D technical organisation.

Project management is a concept increasingly applied to the technical organisation of R&D. The formal structure has to be adapted so that each project is a separate segment. Such a system may be superimposed on the formal structure, the latter acting as a labour pool from which projects are manned. Project management covers, in respect of each major project the following:

1   Defining project objectives and establishing terms of reference.
2   Estimating costs, including any re-estimating required.
3   Planning the project programme and re-timing when necessary.
4   Setting completion and review dates.
5   Appointing a project manager.
6   Choosing the project team.

The project manager is a key man, he is the link between his team and company top management. To enable him to be effective, he should report to the same level as the functional managers, or higher. He is responsible for the success of his project and a major part of his job is to 'sell' the success of the work to top management. Furthermore, the personal commitment given to his project by team members, who no doubt are working only part-time with him and part-time on other projects, will depend to a large extent on how well their work is presented and received at the highest level.

The project management approach to R&D technical organisation has much to recommend it where complex tasks are involved. The main advantages over other methods of dealing with complex tasks are:

1   A team is built up which is related to the job content of the particular task, so that relevant expertise is available to deal with problems.
2   Communication problems are minimized.
3   Accountability for the task is established more easily than if the work were completed in stages by different teams. This leads to conditions in which work is more likely to be completed on schedule.
4   The uncertainty and change inherent in the project-management approach to organisation, is more likely to stimulate interest and provide impetus than with other methods.

There are dangers, but these may be overcome with careful planning. The main one is that the stability of the organisation as a whole may suffer if the formal structure is weakened by project staffing.

3.4.2   R&D administration

The principal function of R&D administrative staff is to free technical personnel, particularly the R&D chief executive, from routine management duties. The complex matter of administration is placed in the hands of those best suited to handle it. A department of research administration may be expected to provide laboratory personnel and equipment, library and information services, data processing facilities and accountancy staff. R&D administration is looked at from the accounting point of view in Chapters 12 and 13.

3.5   COMMUNICATIONS

If the authority structure is the skeleton of R&D organisation, then the communications are the nervous system. This chapter, so far, has been concerned with setting up the R&D organisation. Communications, on the other hand, deal with the flow of information; having the right amount available at the right time and in the right place.

The use of good communications in industry permits the creative ability of the scientist to flourish simultaneously with his work being directed by management towards the achievement of corporate goals.

Owing to the creative and unprogrammed nature of the function the
scientist has substantial influence over the direction and shape which
a project takes. With good communications, management can ensure
that those personal attitudes of the scientist which most influence his
work do so in a manner compatible with the company's best interests.

Successful control of projects depends upon full information being
available at project decision points. Project control is normally exercised by multi-disciplinary committees at three points, as illustrated
below with reference to new product development.

3.5.1 Project control

The approach to project control may be developed along systematic
lines as follows:

1 *Initial go-ahead*   A committee, probably chaired by the chief
executive of the company (or profit centre) and on which R&D has
strong representation, will decide whether a particular concept is
worthy of a feasibility study. The committee members will collectively
bring to bear a blend of experience appropriate to the decision to be
taken. A detailed brief will then be prepared for them, probably by a
planning manager responsible for exploratory work on new product
proposals.

2 *Feasibility study review*   The feasibility study may be reviewed
by the committee that gave the initial go-ahead, by a different committee, or by both. In any event it is desirable that the feasibility
study/review committee(s) should hold an even balance between
R&D and operating functions, and at least one committee member
should be capable of considering the implications of the project for
the company as a whole. The review committee(s) will be advised as
appropriate by market research, by R&D as to technical feasibility
(the applied research function), by the accounts department as to
financial viability, and by production management. A decision will
be taken whether or not to proceed with development work.

3 *The go-ahead decision*   The final decision whether to manufacture
and market the product will be made by a high level committee. The
company chief executive will probably chair the committee if the
project is a major one. This committee will be advised by development engineers on whether the product specifications have been
agreed by the feasibility study review committee, and whether there
are any unresolved technical problems that could interfere with
manufacture and marketing. The latter function will advise on latest

44 sales expectations for the project and on plans for packaging, advertising and promotion. The accounts department will provide product profitability and cash flow forecasts; investment appraisal techniques may be applied if the merits of alternative courses of action are under consideration. The decision whether to go ahead *or* to reconsider *or* abandon will be taken at this stage. This is a vital decision. If £500,000 has been spent on a project it will be difficult to abandon and yet this may be the correct decision.

The difficulties of communicating within and between the R&D function and other disciplines can be simplified by the use of groups or committees. The execution of R&D tasks can be simplified by the use of project teams. Liaison between functions can be simplified by the use of project planning and review committees. However, committees are time-consuming and therefore the proceedings must be timetabled and controlled.

3.6 PERSONAL RELATIONSHIPS IN R&D

Company organisation is based on formal and informal authority structure, and communications bring the structure to life. There remains to be discussed the roles that people play in organisations.
The subject of organisational roles embraces

1   The formal interrelationship of jobs, as determined by the functions allocated to them.
2   The quality of performance of individual job holders.

Together, these these two factors determine the contribution that any one person makes towards corporate objectives. A study of roles is particularly important due to the fact, discussed earlier, that people often have greater scope for self-expression in R&D than in other corporate functions. Organisations should recruit people possessing personal aims and values suited to the organisation's objectives and to the work tasks that these imply.
Management psychologists and behavioural scientists draw a primary distinction between the 'professional' values of scientists and the 'organisational' values of managers. The executive responsible for R&D administration should clearly be drawn from the latter group. The research worker, on the other hand, will be drawn from the former, and recruitment techniques must distinguish between the two. The R&D chief executive, whose main tasks are discussed in the following section, must hold a balanced view.

The role of the chief executive may be summarised as one of establishing and maintaining the R&D function in the forefront of the board's thinking on the corporate future. A list of the main technical tasks is given below (it is assumed that the R&D administration function will take care of other tasks). The list is an adaptation of one given by McLeod [2].

1   Attend board and other general policy meetings.
2   Hold regular discussion with planning and marketing departments.
3   Guide the formulation of research policy.
4   Approve the allocation of development priorities.
5   Study budget proposals and make recommendations to the board or other authority responsible for approving them.
6   Receive reports on any project that has fallen behind its programme and initiate suitable action.
7   Monitor the performance of his staff and the structure of his organisation and initiate changes as required.
8   Ensure the existence of a satisfactory salary structure for technical staff.
9   Interview applicants for senior positions.

Clearly, the R&D chief executive has a key role to play. He must be chosen with care for his technical and personal qualities. Moreover, his remuneration and fringe benefits should compensate him for the substantial contribution he is expected to make towards corporate success.

3.6.2   Motivation of the R&D worker

It was noted above that the R&D worker should be chosen from the behavioural group that possess 'professional' rather than 'organisational' values. A problem exists in that men from the preferred group whem employed in organisations will tend to be orientated towards their profession rather than towards organisational goals. The motivation of these workers will tend therefore to tax the best of chief executives.

The R&D environment differs from company to company, but it is possible nevertheless to list the following requirements for the successful motivation of staff:

1   Close attention to the career development of individual scientists.

Each man should be encouraged to develop his scientific ability and enhance his professional reputation. Employers may achieve this by providing:

a   opportunities for R&D workers to attend scientific conferences in order to further their technical knowledge and develop professional contacts in their field or interests;

b   for each person, progressively more challenging scientific work so that his technical ability is constantly tested and improved;

c   the time and facilities necessary to enable workers to prepare and present technical papers;

d   financial assistance towards membership of appropriate professional bodies.

2   A system of compensation that enables R&D workers to advance their salaries, fringe benefits and status, strictly on the basis of the contribution to the achievement of corporate objectives. This may or may not include the payment of a percentage of patent royalties or comparable direct encouragement to successful scientists.

3   The best possible environment for creative ability. Many R&D workers prefer not to be troubled with routine administrative duties and, therefore, where feasible clerical and accounting work should be given to administrative assistants. However, a minimum level of accountability cannot be avoided even for research workers.

It will be noted that the list represents a careful blend of professional encouragement on the one hand, and an orientation towards corporate objectives on the other.

4
RELATING
R&D ACTIVITY
TO CORPORATE
OBJECTIVES

4.1 CORPORATE OBJECTIVES

There is general acceptance that a company should have specified objectives. These are the formal goals of the business and represent the aims of the board of directors. In broad terms they may cover:

1   Commercial objectives − profit targets, financial stability and satisfactory growth.
2   Collateral objectives − giving satisfaction to customers and employees, as well as to society generally.

These two categories overlap and affect each other.

Going into detail on specific objectives it becomes necessary to stipulate the types of products or services to be manufactured or supplied. This process would also extend into the evolutionary process − is the company to be left to grow haphazardly, or is there to be planned growth? R&D may supply many of the answers required.

There is no standard pattern for success. What these objectives should be are questions that have attracted much attention from management authors such as Ansoff, Argenti and Drucker. It is generally accepted that for a commercial organisation, making a profit or breaking

48   even is the overriding objective, without which all others are meaningless, at least in the long-term.

Corporate objectives will generally include commitments to:

1   Increase the value of the 'risk-bearers' investment in the company.
2   Ensure the continued existence of the company.

These may also be extended to incude fulfilment of social responsibilities.

In planning for the achievement of these objectives, the managers of a company must review the markets they propose to serve and their competitive strengths and weaknesses for doing so. They must also provide a firm foundation of people, products and invested capital to enable it to meet any future changes.

The original writers on corporate planning stressed the need to ask the question 'What business are we in?'. This possibly shows how important innovation can be to many companies. Moreover, since the R&D function often provides one of the mainsprings of growth, it is essential to make sure that the optimum research activity is carried out to produce the results required. A more recent trend has been to rephrase the question to 'What business should we be in?'. This phrase emphasises more than ever the importance of search to the business which relies on growth, innovation and flexibility for successful survival.

4.1.1   R&D objectives

As stressed earlier, a company needs a set of objectives before it can embark on strategic and tactical planning. It is necessary to ask two vital questions:

1   What is the role of R&D in this process?
2   What are to be the objectives for the R&D function?

The role of the function will vary according to the type of business or institution in which it is to be carried out. If a company is operating in a highly competitive environment characterised by the continuous introduction of new products, then the primary role of R&D is clear — to develop new products that will appeal to the consumer, thereby ensuring the competitive viability of the company. Alternatively, a company having monopolistic or oligopolistic status where there are only a *few* important sellers as opposed to one — a monopoly, may regard the function as a speculative side-line, on the look out for further profitable opportunities often possible in competitively restricti situations.

Research and development may be seen to have a vital place in determining the future of a company, with objectives clearly defined to cover overall corporate plans. Despite this, a definition of its role may be substantially influenced by the contribution that the function is

believed to make to the performance of corporate goals. Two views
prevail on the correct approach. First, that there should be a strong
correlation between the amount spent on R&D and the rate of
corporate growth − thus taking the view that the activity has an effect
upon future prosperity directly proportional to the effort expended.
Secondly, that with most companies the function tends to be only
partially effective, which means that a considerable amount of expenditure and effort is wasted, because much of the work, especially on
the research side, is dealing with uncertainties that cannot be quantified.
If these two conflicting views are to be allowed, then clearly a
considerable volume of successful R&D work is required to maintain
or improve the rate of corporate expansion. A statement of R&D
objectives is then an amalgam, comprising an expression of the aims
designed to secure for the company the future appeal of its product(s)
and the efficiency of its production methods, coloured by an interpretation of the function's real ability to contribute to future prosperity. As with any attempt at establishing goals, it amounts to setting
the desirable or ideal objectives and then modifying these in the light
of what experience and/or intuition indicates as reasonable.

4.2 R&D STRATEGY

The strategy developed to attain desired objectives will depend on the
management philosophy and strategy employed by the company as
a whole. It will usually be determined by the following factors:

1 *Technology*   The type of industry and whether it is subject to
   technological or scientific change, including the degree to which
   it is characterised by aggressive competition in terms of products
   and other opportunities.
2 *Corporate strengths and weaknesses*   The overall corporate
   policy and the type of directors or senior managers who hold
   the balance of power within a company. Some companies are
   finance-orientated and therefore tend to have a large number of
   accountants in senior management positions. Others may look
   to engineers for their ideas and impetus in achieving the corporate objectives. Whilst there is no monopoly for any particular
   group of experts, some companies have a research-orientated
   board of directors which feels committed towards a substantial
   level of expenditure. At the other extreme there are companies
   which believe that R&D activities should be kept to an
   absolute minimum.
3 *Information availability*   The effectiveness of management
   information systems in producing data for the board of directors

in developing the R&D programme. R&D as a function is affected by many factors, and whilst the most important might be termed 'technological', relating to new methods of production, improved materials and various other aspects of advanced technology, there are other considerations which will affect the method and scope of the function. Accordingly, a management information system which can provide a full assessment of a company's *external environment* including its legal, social, and economic elements, and its *internal environment,* including utilisation of resources, organisation effectiveness, and cost and pricing structures, can make a highly significant contribution to the development of corporate strategy in general, and R&D strategy in particular.

If R&D is to be an effective force, then company management must recognise the significance of these factors both individually and in aggregate, when developing a suitable strategy. There should be full recognition given to the fact that constraints and limiting factors can play a considerable part in the development of new ideas. Ability to cope will be influenced by information available and managerial skills.

4.2.1   Types of strategy

The specification of R&D strategy, whilst primarily determined by the factors outlined above, is subject to a number of particular influences; but before looking at these, it may be useful to distinguish the different types of strategy. Some writers have suggested the following breakdown:

1   Defensive
2   Offensive
3   Basic

This classification allows directors to appreciate the motive behind a research project. A good idea can be obtained of what these terms mean by reference to Figure 4.1.

It will be seen from this diagram that there are many interacting forces which may be summarised as follows:

1   *Dividend policy* – this will be influenced by the current rate of dividends generally and within industry, and also the economic situation. If there is considerable pressure to pay higher dividends, rather than retain funds, the R&D function may tend to be neglected. (D/O).

2   *Availability of finance and the waiting list of project proposals requiring attention.* (O).
3   *The danger of obsolescence and change in fashion of the products.* (D)
4   *Competition within the industry* — this affects the amount of R&D required to keep level with or ahead of competitors (D/O/B)
5   *Competition from other industries on substitute products.* (O/B)
6   *Availability of resources to develop and exploit R projects that can be successful.* (D/O)
7   *Manpower available for carrying out R&D projects.* (D/O/B)
8   *The company's policy and strategy on the achievement of its corporate objectives and whether it prefers to lead the field or to follow the leader within the industry.* (D/O/B)

All these factors will be considered in so far as they affect the specific R&D programme within a company. Their impact upon the three main types of R&D will tend to differ, and this is indicated by the letters given after the descriptions above. The key is 'D' for *defensive* research, 'O' for *offensive* research, and 'B' for *basic* research. The pressures from these forces may result in requests for larger allocations in the R&D budget. Although there is no evidence to confirm the fact, it is usually thought that the basic budget is determined by the minimum amount which should be spent to keep the business going as a viable concern.

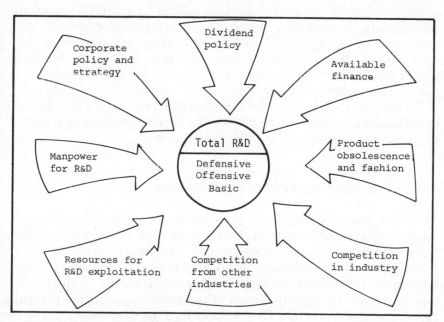

Figure 4.1   The forces influencing total R&D

However, there are other considerations which although linked to this level, tend to have wider implications; in some cases they are not strictly economic factors.

4.2.2   Minimum and maximum levels of R&D activity

A major problem in planning R&D activity is to find the appropriate level of expenditure which will achieve the stated objectives.

A company, having analysed the nature and problems of the industry in which it operates, should be able to calculate the minimum commitment that it must make to the function. This minimum, sometimes known as the *threshold level,* is the amount required to provide adequate manpower and facilities, and to maintain contact with outside research and other bodies working in the particular field. This threshold level is the smallest amount that can be spent to make R&D a worthwhile commercial venture.

Under conditions of resource scarcity, it is usual to find that the maximum commitment made to R&D depends upon the availability of resources as a whole, and the extent to which rationing is applied to allocate those resources between competing interests. If capital rationing is necessary, then the maximum allocation obtained by the function will be a direct reflection of its ability to show that a greater return may be had from investing in R&D than in alternative areas. A criticism of British research is centred around its inability to convert findings into commercial propositions — that it is sometimes regarded as the poor relation of other competing commercial activities is not surprising. Where resources are not scarce, then the maximum allocation is that amount which the activity regards as necessary for the optimum solution to its problems.

Ultimately, the amount to be spent will generally be a compromise between the maximum requested by the Director of Research and the minimum as indicated by the threshold level.

4.2.3   The importance of finance availability

As will be shown in Chapter 6, there are many methods for determining the amount that should be set aside each year. These are often a percentage of the profits being earned, or a figure calculated by reference to a percentage of some other factor such as sales or even total costs. It is sometimes suggested that R&D should be the first item to be cut when profits begin to fall and certainly if the percentage on profits is taken, then it follows that the function may well be cut back when profits start to decline. However, the same comment

could be made about administration, training, and other areas with 53
no direct link with the amount produced and sold within a particular
period. There is no evidence to show that R&D budgets are usually cut
back any further or quicker than those of other functional areas.

Except as a guide for determining how much a company can afford,
a fixed percentage of some figure such as profit, hardly gives a sensible
guide as to how much should be spent on R&D. The fact remains
though, that if a company continues to operate successfully within
the limits laid down by this approach, then there is little reason to
advocate an alternative. The amount of research effort should be
determined in the first place by the service required to keep the company operating at an optimum level, and secondly by the amount which
it can afford at a specific time.

Even when information is available on trends and technological
development, it is still important to consider the financial constraints
that exist. In any event, there will be many decisions to be backed by
judgment.

4.3 TECHNIQUES FOR LONG-RANGE R&D PLANNING

For an R&D programme to be developed, there should be reference to
the time scale in which a company operates. This may be determined
by the life of fixed assets, or the production cycle, or by some other
factor which has an important influence on the operations. There is
need to recognise this time scale so that corporate planning can cover
the appropriate long-term period (perhaps twenty years or more), as
well as the short term which is usually broken down into two periods
– the business cycle, between two and five years, and the budget
period which may be a year or six months.

The sales forecast is generally the starting point for determining
how much can be sold and therefore the capacity at which a company
can operate. Accordingly, this forecast should always be in the fore-
ground of any planning activity, whether of short or long term. The
importance of technological forecasting should also be kept in mind
because it can have a considerable bearing on the function.

There are many excellent books dealing with the problems and
methods of business forecasting, but they usually emphasise that
intuition and judgment must continue to play a considerable part
in any predictive exercise. Despite this fact, there is much to be said
for using all available *objective* measures to justify any forecasts which
are made.

Usually, the basic methods used for forecasting are as follows:

1   *Executive opinions*   The opinions of salesmen, sales executives

and others are obtained and where appropriate these are modified to allow for government legislation, changes in patterns of spending and other known facts. Appropriate changes in policy may also be incorporated into the forecasts which have been derived from this method. This method encourages participative management and, therefore, brings to bear the experience of those who are selling the products or services. The main problems are personal bias and possibly a lack of knowledge on the broader issues which affect company policy.

2 *Trend analysis* With this method, trends are plotted which consider all relevant factors. Changes which have taken place in the past are usually assumed to continue into the immediate future. There is *some* truth in the assertion that: 'The past is no guide to the future'. However, properly used figures which show trends can be of immense value for assessing future trends.

3 *Correlation analysis of sales and other variables* With this approach the idea is to select some factor which shows a marked correlation with the level of business achieved by the company. Generally such time 'leads' or 'lags' as can be identified are brought into the correlation analysis. Indices used have included disposable income, gross national product, population, and the output of specific industries, such as the number of cars produced.

4 *Compiling economic models* The building of forecasting models is now an accepted method for determining long- and short-term plans. The factors likely to affect the forecast are established and a model then built which incorporates all essential requirements. These are expressed mathematically and the model is validated by carrying out tests using historical data. Once the foundation is laid, a model can become 'predictive', thus enabling forecasts to be made.

In practice, a combination of two or more of these approaches will generally be necessary. Refinements may also be introduced, some of which are considered below.

4.3.1 Technological forecasting

Technological forecasting has developed considerably in recent years. With the growth in advanced technology, it has become necessary to consider the pace of development and whether the various factors affecting progress have an impact on related industries or companies within the same industry. Unfortunately, there are difficulties associated with applying what is quite a complex technique. Apart from the sales from one industry having an impact on another, there have been

cases where a product has been developed by a company not concerned or even assoicated with the relevant area. Examples can be seen
in the development of polaroid photography, xerography and man-
made fibres, none of which originated from the photographic, office
machinery and textile industries, respectively. Because of these
'haphazard' developments, it generally means that technological forecasting should be viewed in a broad fashion rather than being limited
to a single company or industry. When this is done, the horizons
become so wide that uncertainty may be increased to a critical level.
A major problem is that the facilities required for a particular product
or service have tended to develop at a much later stage than the main
product. This is seen in the case of aircraft, where the development of
aircraft conveyor equipment for handling passengers and freight has
tended to lag behind what is necessary for the larger and more powerful modern aircraft now in service.

The same type of 'backwardness' can also be seen in the network of
roads, garages, motels and other facilities required to back up the
explosive development of the motor car industry.

A different area of development is in the educational field where
colleges and universities have expanded at a tremendous rate. This has
also been linked with an acceleration in the size of disposable incomes
which people find themselves able to spend on recreational facilities as
well as the necessities of life. With improved education and more
purchasing power, it is inevitable that demand changes and thus affects
the pattern of spending.

There appears to be no generally accepted definition of 'technological
forecasting'. That its application should be wide is acknowledged, but
the precise objectives are not clear especially when viewed from the
point of view of a single company. How far the latter should go with
limited resources is always a difficult question to answer. What is
required is a definition of the areas to be covered and the maximum
possible use of external sources of information, and exploitation of
developments by other companies.

Technological forecasting adopts a systematic approach to the
assessment of the effects of development of methods, machinery,
scientific discoveries and other inventions affecting the R&D
function, so that resources can be channelled in the direction most
likely to achieve corporate objectives. Thus there is a link from the past
to the present, and into the future, to see what development are taking
place and how they can be profitably exploited.

4.4   INTEGRATION OF R&D FUNCTION

The R&D objectives were discussed earlier in this chapter. Their achievement requires that the plan should be long term — the precise duration depending on the individual company's circumstances. The long term plans are then broken down into, say, two to five year plans with a further sub-division covered by the annual budget.

In drawing up these plans, consideration must be given to the impact of one function on another. There must be consultation at and between different levels of management; namely, board members, general management, divisional and functional management, including production, marketing, administration, and R&D.

The impact of R&D on the other functions requires special attention. Where a business is large enough, the appointment of a manager to integrate or coordinate the strategic plan so as to allow for overlapping requirements, will be essential. The production function may have certain views regarding the impact of a particular project, but these may be different from those held by the senior marketing managers. If the R&D project is to be successful for the company as a whole, then coordination is vital.

In planning R&D work, consideration should be given to the effect of different projects on the profit potential of the company. Change can often result in heavy costs, and yet, unless there is innovation, a company may stagnate with a result that its growth potential is never fully realised. There may be pressure from the marketing function to introduce better designs and cheaper products. Often these are essentially short-term projects that will bring about an improvement in sales in the current year, but may not have a lasting effect. Whilst these projects can be essential, so should be the development of long-term ideas for new products to expand the company as a whole or to replace old products with a limited life. In short, a director of R&D should be strong enough to ensure that he is carrying out a balanced programme which meets both short- and long-term corporate objectives.

4.5 CONTROL IN THE R&D FUNCTION

Although control is not a popular concept, especially with those who are controlled, it is vital to have constraints or limitations on the amount of money which is to be spent. Furthermore, if plans are made a watch should be kept to ensure that these are achieved. Failure to achieve targets suggests inefficiency on the part of the managers concerned. These should be identified and corrective action taken to avoid any repetition in the future. Control therefore, is a major part of the management function, and if it is to be carried out effectively, it requires a clear definition of responsibilities, and authority to take action when matters are not proceeding according to plan.

Because of the importance of R&D, it is now common practice for the director responsible to be a member of the board of directors. This is essential for several reasons, such as:

1   Importance of R&D in achieving corporate objectives.
2   Necessity for a channel of communication to the highest level in a company, so that the function can be given its rightful place in the organisation. (Without boardroom backing, there can be little hope of achieving an effective R&D programme.)
3   Coordination of the functional activities mentioned earlier will only be achieved when the R&D director can discuss matters with directors in charge of other functions.

It is common practice for the director in charge of R&D to report to the chairman or to the managing director. Provided the programme is approved and major projects are also given approval, it is usual for the director to have considerable freedom to make changes necessary in utilizing the resources, provided his budget is not exceeded. Even on the latter, there may be some flexibility — certain companies have a contingency fund to allow the R&D director to pursue some technological breakthrough so that it can be exploited as quickly as possible.

4.5.1   The impact of the organisation

The general principles relating to organisation are covered in Chapter 3. In connection with coordination and control, the type of organisation employed can have an impact on these two important functions. In this connection, the planning of the organisation structure will require attention to be paid to whether the concern is with:

1   Basic research.
2   Applied research.
3   Development.

Often the basic research projects are long term, and once started, their coordination and control may be simple. Provided the objectives fit in with the overall corporate objectives, this type of research can continue from year to year. On the control side, it is generally necessary merely to ensure that the annual amount budgeted is not exceeded in the period, and that it is regularly reviewed and reported upon to ensure that it is reasonable.

Applied research and development projects usually have more specific objectives and therefore can be subjected to more stringent control. If the expected results are not forthcoming, these projects can be abandoned. They are usually of a medium- or short-term duration because they have reached the stage where results are to be expected.

Because of these differences looked at on a time basis, there may be merit in dividing the organisation so that the basic research is separated from the other two activities. With development, technical considerations may call for much of the work to be done where there is a factory, so that the necessary plant and machinery is available for test runs, building prototypes, and other necessary work. This may call for a certain amount of decentralisation.

How far R&D should be centralised is a matter for conjecture. Common practice indicates that a high degree of centralisation is preferred, but certain types of work are best performed at the operating units. A coordinator can then ensure there is not too much duplication, and in addition, that one part of the company benefits from the work done in the other. Even where all the work cannot be centralised, there are certain administrative functions which may be carried out at head office, or at some other central place. This is particularly important when personnel have to be transferred to different parts of the world to engage in the work.

4.5.2   The task-force approach

When considering the appropriate organisation for R&D, there are many variations which may be used. As shown in Chapter 3, the conventional approach suggests a director responsible for R&D with a manager reporting to him for each major activity. These managers in turn are given the necessary facilities and personnel, and are held responsible for the work carried out. This approach is easily understood and when used effectively can bring satisfactory results.

An alternative approach is to use the 'task-force method'. A team of workers is set up under a senior manager or director with a view to achieving results quickly by concentrating on a particular problem. Advantages claimed for this approach are:

1   Techniques, skills and other requirements can be brought together in the appropriate quantities and at the right time.
2   Because the task force has specific objectives, it can concentrate on these without being held back by day-to-day problems.
3   Results can be obtained quicker because the team has top-management backing, and it is known by all managers that results are expected quickly.
4   Because results come quicker, it follows that errors which may not emerge for some time with the conventional approach, are

brought to light before much damage has been done.

5   The task force is brought together with definite ends in view,
     and its work will cease when these have been achieved, so there
     should be no tendency for empire building.

The approach for setting up a task force varies from one company
to another but generally there will be a clear definition of the
objectives and the target date for achievement. The approach demands
the application of a wide range of skills with no restrictions imposed
by way of functional barriers, and the task force leaders must be able
to call upon personnel from different functions such as engineering,
marketing, production, or administration.

The task force is not necessarily a part of the formal organisation
structure of the company, although provision for setting up the
informal unit should be made when the organisation is considered.
Because of the informal nature of the task force, it is essential that the
results obtained from its work are fed back to the director of research,
and where appropriate to the board of directors.

4.6 SUMMARY

Relating R&D to corporate objectives is a complex topic, but one
that must be firmly grasped, particularly by those whose future
prosperity is not guaranteed by the continued exploitation of past
innovation.

The essence of the relationship is *interactive*, i.e. whilst corporate
objectives are the prime determinants of R&D objectives and strategy,
R&D capability will always influence the validity of corporate goals so
long as resource scarcity persists. The activity must be planned,
organised and controlled with strict reference to the shorter-term
objectives and strategy of the company, but simultaneously with the
express purpose and facility of generating new ideas which will
contribute significantly to determining longer-term strategy and even
primary objectives.

5
PLANNING THE
R&D PROGRAMME

5.1   INTRODUCTION

If the definition of R&D objectives and strategy is designed to determine the role of the function, then planning the programme is the
prerequisite of action necessary to fulfil that role. Unless planning
of the programme is explicitly derived from the declared purpose
of the function, then chance will play a large part in determining
the extent to which corporate objectives are ultimately attained.

The object of this chapter is, therefore, to explain the method
by which ideas postulated as meriting investigation are screened,
analysed and finally selected or rejected. More perhaps has been
written in the field of R&D on the techniques of project selection
than on any other subject, and nothing is more conspicuous in the
majority of these writings than their lack of appreciation that the
exclusive use of any one technique is usually dangerous. However,
it is refreshing to note from the contributions written by R&D
practitioners that they are aware of this — although some appear
to be obsessed by the desire to incorporate every conceivable
criterion of suitability in a single, all embracing, measure!

This chapter seeks to highlight the main problems in planning
a programme, and will discuss briefly the more important techniques

available for evaluating individual projects and project portfolios.
It will not deal with the operational planning of projects except in
so far as this precedes selection appraisal.

5.2 THE STAGES OF PLANNING

Planning for the future activity of an operation whose 'commodity'
is uncertainty must, by its nature, be flexible, not only in the
sense of being able to handle a diverse collection of ideas randomly
generated from a wide range of sources, but also capable of reacting
to change imposed upon a programme of work already started.

A system of R&D programme planning must therefore be broadly
based and of dynamic form if it is not to become a strait-jacket,
unable to accommodate opportunities whose potential might have
dramatic consequences for the firm.

The main stages of programme preparation are:

1   Review of current activities.
2   Screening of all suggested research ideas.
3   Appraisal of 'candidate' proposals.
4   Selection of a portfolio of 'qualified' projects.

These steps will be discussed in this order and the principal techniques
available for each will be explained at the relevant stages.

5.3 REVIEW OF CURRENT ACTIVITIES

Just as questions of the type 'What business are we in?' require investigation in the corporate planning process, so the planning of an R&D
programme demands a critical assessment of the work currently being
conducted. Current research projects should be the subject of regular
monitoring procedures incorporated in systems of budgetary and
progress control, but it will be necessary, at least once a year, to take
an overall view of activities. This review should form not only an
essential part of the control mechanism, but also be the first step in
the annual planning exercise, and be designed to answer such questions
as:

1   Does the collection of projects – the portfolio – currently being
     undertaken, concentrate undue attention in any particular area to
     the detriment of any other area?
2   Is the portfolio as a whole too risky, i.e. is there on balance,
     excessive activity in areas known to be, or likely to become highly

unpredictable in terms of outcome?
3   Is the proportion of future resources committed to projects
     already started unduly high or low when set against the likely
     requirements of new research proposals?
4   Are the research projects being undertaken so significant in terms
     of likely success that all the resources available in the immediate
     future should be devoted to them, to the exclusion of any new
     proposals?

   In the course of any analysis conducted on these lines, R&D
management should be aiming to form a view of the adequacy of the
existing programme in fulfilling its defined role. Upon completion
of the analysis, a picture should emerge of any gap or shortfall that
exists between the objectives which it is anticipated will be achieved
by the existing programme of research, and the desired objectives of
the future programme(s).

   The purpose of screening, analysing and selecting new research
proposals is to fill that gap or shortfall and, of course, to look at these
within the broad framework of the current portfolio.

5.4   SCREENING OF SUGGESTED RESEARCH IDEAS

The need for a flexible planning system is essential in dealing with a
diverse collection of ideas randomly generated from a wide range of
sources. The numbers and types of sources will depend on the circumstances of the company, the nature of the research establishment, its
financial backing, the key personnel and other relevant factors which
affect the 'links' which can be established.

5.4.1   Sources of research ideas

Generally speaking, companies operating in one of the manufacturing
sectors will derive research ideas from any or all of the following source

1   The R&D department.
2   The corporate planning department.
3   Customers; direct, or via marketing or service functions.
4   The production function.
5   The quality control function.
6   The marketing function, including:
     a   product planning;
     b   market research;
     c   advertising and promotion.
7   Government agencies, universities and consultants.

TABLE 5.1 Sources of research ideas

Research staff	60%
Marketing staff	17%
Customers, including	
Government agencies	9%
General management	9%
Others, including production,	
universities & consultants	5%
	100%

The sources of research ideas indicated by recent surveys are shown in
Table 5.1. In the interests of clarity a list of surveys has not been included. Rather they have been lumped together since the purpose of the
table is to show tendencies rather than precise figures.

Predictably, the R&D function itself is responsible for producing
the overall majority of new proposals, but it is interesting to note that
over one quarter arise from marketing and customer sources. This
distribution will vary from industry to industry, and company to company and, if more attention is paid to the idea of 'marketing-oriented'
management, it is likely that analysis over a period would reveal an
increasing contribution of ideas originating in the marketing and allied
functions. In those situations where the sources of ideas are diverse
and numerous, some form of pro-forma statement explaining each idea
will assist the screening stage of programme planning.

5.4.2   The number of research ideas

The second feature of the screening process concerns the volume of
ideas emanating from each source. It is characteristic of R&D that
only a small proportion of research ideas lead to commercial propositions, and some investigations have indicated that less than one fifth
even reach the stage of a preliminary laboratory appraisal. In the
face of these odds the screening process must be rapid and efficient,
but it must also maintain a high level of objectivity if it is to serve its
purpose.

5.4.3   Criteria for 'pass' or 'fail'

Each idea should be examined by managers, including R&D senior
management, against a series of broadly defined strategic qualifications,

as follows:

1   Is it likely to be within the existing or future technological capability of the research unit?
2   Does it conflict with corporate attitudes to environmental, social or political matters?
3   Does intuition or assessment suggest its commercial viability?
4   Has it already been investigated, either internally or externally, and what was the outcome?
5   Does its development and exploitation appear to be broadly within the financial means of the company?

Many more questions will spring readily to mind, but the requisite number at this preliminary stage will ultimately be determined by reference to:

a   The number of ideas to be examined.
b   The resources and information available to make detailed appraisals of 'strategically qualified' proposals.

One final point remains. If the chief executive of the R&D function is to ensure that the screening process fulfills its purpose, then he should encourage *all* potential sources of research ideas and to submit suggestions on those which appear good prospects. Fresh ideas are vital, for without them, the screening process, however efficient, will not serve the best interests of the company.

5.5   APPRAISAL OF 'CANDIDATE' PROPOSALS

Proposals submitted for detailed appraisal should be relatively few in number, as their investigation is likely to consume much time and effort. As mentioned earlier, the circumstances of the individual company will largely dictate the volume of research ideas having any potential. For instance, if a company is operating in a narrowly defined market, it may generate only a few research ideas with little desire or ability to diversify. It may therefore find it unnecessary to adopt an initial screening approach, but instead to subject each individual research idea to vigorous examination.

5.5.1   The purpose of proposal investigation

The purpose of proposal investigation is essentially twofold:

1   To identify projects that, having passed the screening phase, do not measure up to the criteria of acceptability established

by the company, so that these may be eliminated.
2　To evaluate the remaining proposals against the same set of
criteria, in order ultimately to select a suitable portfolio of
projects for research.

The criteria used in the screening process were defined in fairly
broad terms, thus paying limited attention to specific features or
attributes of individual proposals. The selection phase which follows
is designed to investigate each proposal in as much detail as is
feasible. This may be an expensive task as it will mean pursuing all
available avenues of information. The latter helps to minimise the
risk that management runs when deciding on those uncertain courses
of action to which it proposes to commit itself. It is not intended to
discuss the criteria for selection at this stage, as these are outlined
in Section 5.5.3 below.

5.5.2　The nature of proposal investigation

From an examination of Figure 5.1 it will be seen that the problem
may be viewed as being three-dimensional, *viz:*

1　The type of investigation (qualitative/quantitative).
2　The attributes of the project (individual/relative).
3　Inter-project objectives (similar/dissimilar).

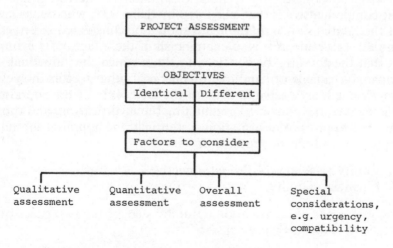

Figure 5.1　Investigation of projects

The type of investigation adopted will depend primarily on the quantity and quality of information required on each project. It will also depend on the availability of technical expertise and facilities such as data processing, which are necessary for many of the present selection techniques. These two factors will determine both the extent and balance of quantitative and qualitative assessment applied to each research project.

The nature of the investigation will also be affected by the attributes of each project *per se,* i.e. whether in their own right they appear to merit exploitation, and by their appeal relative to a proposed portfolio of projects. In this latter respect, the degree to which projects are interdependent is important. The manner in which the selection of one project affects the selection of another, both in terms of resource utilisation and final outcome should not be overlooked. Finally, the appraisal system may require the facility to distinguish between projects competing to satisfy the same corporate objectives and those which are motivated from individual preferences.

5.5.3   The criteria used in project appraisal

The degree to which any given research proposal can be investigated is determined by the availability of relevant information and the ability to use that information meaningfully. The volume and quality of information obtained will depend upon the number and nature of criteria which have to be considered.

Authors and practitioners have suggested a variety of criteria indicators covering the likely functions that affect R&D. Perhaps the most comprehensive is that suggested by Seiler [3], who considers that the factors shown in Table 5.2 should be considered in project appraisal. Desirable as it is to examine all of these factors, it is important that the appraisal be confined to those which the individual company is capable of handling. Inclusion of other factors, however attractive, will only serve to damage the credibility of the appraisal in the eyes of the personnel conducting the investigation, and those requested to provide information. Essentially the appraisal should justify a project on the grounds of its:

1   Ability to achieve a desired objective.
2   Financial viability.

These two areas of justification naturally suggest the two types of assessment show in Figure 5.1, *viz:*

1   Qualitative.
2   Quantitative.

TABLE 5.2 Performance indicators in R&D

Technical factors	1 Availability of the necessary scientific skills 2 Adequacy of research facilities (the need for employing consultants, research associations, etc.) 3 Adequacy of support manpower 4 Utilisation of present skills 5 Probability of technical success 6 Technical approach required to reach a solution
Research direction and balance	1 Compatability of company objectives 2 Compatability of long-term research objectives 3 Maintenance of research balance by products 4 Maintenance of balance between the intermediate and long-range introduction of new products
Timing of research	1 Timing of research completion 2 Timing of development completion 3 Timing of market development 4 Timing of research in relation to competitors' efforts
Stability	1 Prominence of the market 2 Possibility of a captive market 3 Stability in a depression 4 Stability in time of war or shifts in defense spending 5 Difficulty in substitution or copying
Position factor	1 Effect on sales of other product lines 2 Effect on vertical or horizontal integration resulting from raw material usage 3 Possibility of an exclusive raw material purchasing position
Growth factors	1 Export possibilities 2 Possibility of changes or shifts in industry of which this product can take advantage 3 Possibility of a family of products growing from the research 4 Possibility of a substantial future growth in size 5 Diversification
Marketability factor	1 Market potential in immediate future 2 Market potential in long-range future 3 Compatability with current and long-range marketing objectives 4 Competitive environment 5 Promotional requirements 6 Adaptability to present distribution methodology and resources 7 Volume price effects on present products 8 Relationships to Government legislation 9 Compatability with company's present customer make-up 10 Service requirements for product guarantee or upkeep

Continued overleaf

	11	Variations of styles required
	12	Compatability with the company's present reputation in the market
Production factors	1	Compatabilities of production facilities
	2	Utilisation of familiar production processes
	3	Freedom from hazards
	4	Availability of manpower
Financial factors	1	Expected increase in profits
	2	Expected new capital outlays for equipment
	3	Expected cost to complete the project
	4	Expected cost to complete the development
	5	Expected rate of return on invested capital
Protection	1	Possibility of a patent
	2	Unique character of the product or process
	3	The need for continuing defensive research in respect of known areas of competitors' work

5.5.4   Qualitative project assessment

Pure qualitative assessment, whilst helpful in building up a complete picture of the utility of an individual project, is often unfortunately unsatisfactory for comparing projects, because it lacks an objective standard by which to judge a project as good, bad, or indifferent.

Attempts have been made to overcome this problem by employing certain quasi-quantitative techniques. These generally provide for assessing qualitative properties on a numerical scale of subjective probability. For example, a potential product proposed for research might be ranked as 4 on a scale 1 to 5 for the attribute 'difficulty of substitution of copying'. This would imply that it is highly unlikely that the product would be copied — though not impossible. This process may be extended to consider a number of attributes in order to build up a qualitative project profile, an example which is given in Figure 5.2

The profile enables R&D management to obtain at a glance a general 'feel' for the project's outcome — in the example given, 'fair' to 'good'. It also allows appreciation of the spread of risk inherent in the project. In this example, whilst the concensus view is optimistic, there is a full 'spread' of expected outcomes between 'very poor' and 'very good'. If the company prefers to adopt a conservative policy in terms of risk acceptance, it might reject this project in preference to one which showed a greater concentration in the 'fair' region of the profile.

This form of analysis may be developed to produce an index of acceptability, as shown in Figure 5.2. The example given shows an unweighted index based simply upon the numerical ranking of each

PROJECT DESCRIPTION: Development of tin alloy	Ref.No. TA 1234				
	Very poor	Poor	Fair	Good	Very good
	①	②	③	④	⑤
TECHNICAL FACTORS:					
Probability of technical success			✓		
Utilisation of present skills					✓
RESEARCH DIRECTION AND BALANCE:					
Compatability with company objectives				✓	
Maintenance of research balance by products		✓			
STABILITY:					
Possibility of a captive market			✓		
Stability in a depression			✓		
Difficulty of substitution or copying				✓	
GROWTH FACTORS:					
Possibility of a family of products		✓			
Diversification	✓				
PROTECTION:					
Possibility of a patent				✓	
ACCEPTABILITY INDEX 31	1	4	9	12	5

Prepared by: J. Smith   Approved by: T. James

Date: 31|12|72   Date: 15/1/73

Figure 5.2 Project qualitative profile

factor. Further refinement may be introduced by applying different weights to each factor in order to reflect their perceived relative importance. The company may consider 'stability' to be of such over-riding importance that all scores for that factor should merit double the significance of any other factor. Thus, a 'fair' score for this factor would justify six points as against three for all the others.

There are many variations on this theme, the prime objective of which is to produce indicators of project attractiveness comparable with, for example, return on capital employed or payback duration expressed in years. However, it must be emphasised that as these methods depend for their effectiveness upon subjective assessments of likely outcome, any statistical inference derived from comparison of acceptability indices must be made with extreme caution.

5.5.5 Quantitative project assessment

Many of the techniques employed in the financial evaluation of R&D projects stem from the body of knowledge developed for the appraisal of investment opportunities generally. Much of this knowledge is derived from the concept of discounted cash flow (DCF) and from mathematical modelling techniques, such as Monte-Carlo simulation. Before the advent of these techniques, measures such as 'payback period' and 'average return on capital employed' were used. These and other methods will be discussed after examining some of the problems they share in common.

The value of an opportunity, say to invest in a programme of R&D is the difference between its attributable benefits and costs. Therefore the fundamental problem common to any appraisal of a given opportunity is *forecasting* those benefits and costs. Certain attributes are of a qualitative type which can and must be evaluated as such, and if the ultimate objective of the firm is to make a profit, then it is essential to consider all investment opportunities, which include R&D, in terms of their contribution to profits. Thus the prerequisite of financial appraisal techniques is an estimate of the cash flows applicable to the opportunity under examination.

In the first instance this will necessitate the compilation of a forecast of likely sales revenues or, in the case of a proposal to improve a production process, cost savings. It is likely that the first estimate will rely substantially on guess work, but this may be subsequently refined on the basis of, say, a market research exercise. Given an estimate of product volumes, then production management in con-junction with cost accounting personnel should be able to forecast product costs and capital requirements, in terms of cash outflows.

Depending on the outcome of these investigations, R&D personnel will develop an outline operational plan to determine the duration and resource requirements of the proposed line of research.

This brief discussion disguises the complexities in the actual work, but its purpose is to underline the all-embracing approach that is demanded by the available appraisal techniques.

Three problems merit examination at this stage. The premise upon which project appraisal is based is that of the marginal or incremental contribution which an investment opportunity makes to the existing business. The objective therefore is to examine the effects of the investment when hypothetically superimposed upon the business. Herein lies a problem. Accepting the difficulties of predicting the external growth effects for the firm, how is the impact *within* the firm to be anticipated? For example, what is the likely addition, if any, to fixed costs by acceptance of a particular research project? Likely to be of greater significance, if the project becomes a commercial proposition, is the effect that a new product will have on the market for the company's existing products. The contribution of a different sales mix may radically alter, favourably or otherwise, the long-term profitability.

This latter point prompts a second problem; namely, what is the period over which the effects of an implemented proposal will be considered? Chapter 9, which discusses the evaluation of R&D effectiveness, considers this matter in some detail, but it resolves essentially into the need to specify an horizon whatever the criterion for its determination. Preferably the horizon will be the predicted end of the life cycle for the product under examination, but unless extensive experience is obtained in monitoring product life cycles, it may be necessary to set an artificial horizon, say five years hence. It will be seen later that 'payback' and allied techniques may, under certain circumstances, obviate this problem.

Finally, the timing of cash flows may be critical to the viability of a proposed project. Exponents of DCF are the first to stress that cash flows acquire differing values according to the times at which they are experienced — these being a function of the cost of capital to the firm. Again the predicted profile of the product life cycle will be valuable in assessing the impact of time upon the value of future cash flows, but the problems of accurate prediction still apply. Timing may have considerable bearing upon the extent to which inflationary pressures diminish the real value of future cash flows.

5.6.6 Quantitative appraisal techniques

There are numerous techniques and indicators which have been developed to appraise investment opportunities. Some are more

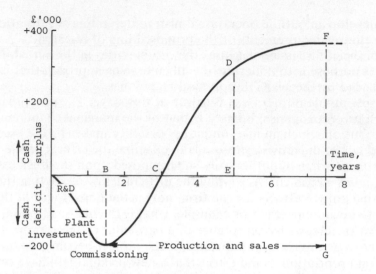

Figure 5.3 Forecast net cash flow profile (cumulative)

popular than others, some more easily implemented than others, and
some are more suitable in particular situations than others. This book
will not attempt to cover all, as they are adequately documented in a
variety of journals and textbooks, but will concentrate attention on
the following:

1   Payback period.
2   Equivalent maximum investment period.
3   Interest recovery period.
4   Average return on investment.
5   Net present value.
6   Internal rate of return.

1   Payback period   This method, as with most of the alternatives,
requires the preparation of a cash flow forecast over time. It is convenient though not essential, to represent the forecast graphically, as
shown in Figure 5.3. It will be seen that the payback point occurs
where the cumulative net cash flow line changes from negative to
positive, indicating a payback period of three years. Thus it is expected fully to recover all outlays within three years – an indication
of inherent risk.

2   Equivalent maximum investment period   This measure indicates
the effective period over which the maximum investment of capital is
considered at risk. It is obtained by expressing the area of cumulative
net cash deficit (area OACBO in Figure 5.3) a multiple of the maximum
investment of capital (BA) – in this case approximately 1.7 years.

3 Interest recovery period   This indicates how long it takes to recover the cost of permanent and working capital invested over the
payback period. It is obtained by examining the cash profile after
the payback point and establishing that point in time where the
cumulative surplus to date equates with the cumulative deficit over
the payback period, *viz.* area OACBO in Figure 5.3. In the example,
this point occurs approximately five years from inception, i.e. two
years after the payback period. It also serves as an indication of the
rate at which the growth phase of the product life cycle is occurring.

4 Average return on investment   This is probably the most popular
of all measures used to portray the expected profitability of an investment proposal. It is found by expressing the total of all profits
(or cost savings) expected from the investment, as a percentage of
total capital employed in the investment. Referring again to Figure
5.3, total profits are found from the line FG and capital invested
from the line AB. The ratio expressed as an annual return is therefore:

$$\left(\frac{FG}{AG}\right) \times \left(\frac{100}{AB}\right) = \left(\frac{560}{6}\right) \times \left(\frac{100}{190}\right) = 49.1\%$$

The assumption has been made, on the lines mentioned earlier,
that as the cash flow profile cannot be predicted to the end of
the product life cycle, an arbitrary cut-off point has been established
seven and a half years after inception. For comparative purposes, it
may be necessary to apply this cut-off point to all competing projects; however, it could be argued that a project with a predictable
cash flow over a ten year period should be treated as such, as this
constitutes a marked advantage over a project of shorter predictable
duration.

Useful though the four methods, (1) to (4) above, are, they do not
take account of the time value of money. In other words, they do not
recognise the value that each annual net cash flow has in terms of the
income that it may earn if re-invested in the business. Thus the present value of a positive cash flow five years hence is that sum which,
together with income accumulated thereon at the rate earned by the
company, will equal the future value of that cash flow. The following
two methods attempt to overcome this limitation.

5 Net present value (NPV)   This technique rests on the premise
that there is a certain cost attached to the capital which a company
uses to invest in income-earning ventures. The cost may be an arbit-
rarily defined figure, for example 10 per cent, though it is preferably
defined by specific reference to the company's sources of capital;

for example, Ordinary shares, loan stock or bank overdraft. This cost is used to arrive at the present discounted worth of future cash flows, on the assumption that it is the minimum rate of return that the company must earn to meet the cost of the finance used for the investment generating the cash flows.

6   *An illustration*   A certain venture requires investment of £100 which once made is regarded as lost. The cost of that capital is 10 per cent per annum. The investment may generate a once and for all positive cash flow of £100 in either:

a   the year of investment; or
b   the fifth year following investment.

In alternative (*a*), the project breaks even in the year of investment with the opportunity of re-investing the £100 inflow for the period of five years, at a compound rate of 10 per cent per annum.
If alternative (*b*) is adopted, having an inflow of £100 expected to occur after a period of five years, the opportunity of further investment of that inflow, over the five year period, is foregone. The equivalent present value of this alternative, at the year of investment, is therefore approximately £62, which, together with compound interest at the rate of 10 per cent per annum for five years, represents the inflow of £100 obtained through alternative (*a*).
Clearly, alternative (*a*) is preferable to (*b*) as the present values of each are £100 and £62, respectively.
Once the annual net cash flows, including capital and revenues receipts and expenditures, have been predicted for the project under review, these are discounted back to present values using the discount rate (cost of capital) for the company. By summing these present values, the project will have either a positive or negative NPV. If positive, the project will be profitable, and if negative, the converse; provided that cash flow expectations are realised. Comparison of the magnitudes of NPVs for competing projects will indicate the sequence in which the projects should be accepted, in order to maximise corporate profitability.

7   *Internal rate of return (IRR)*   This method is a variation on the theme of DCF which endeavours to overcome that arbitrary feature of the NPV method; namely, establishing a suitable discount rate. Its objective is to find that rate of interest which will equate the present value of the cash outflows of an investment project with the present value of the cash inflows generated by that project. The rate may be found by trial and error. If by using a certain rate the project flows show a positive NPV, then the rate may be progressively raised until

NPV reduced to nil. Alternatively, having calculated the NPVs obtained by two rates, one of which is expected to be above the IRR, i.e. negative NPV, and one below, i.e. positive NPV, the IRR may be exactly calculated by graphical interpolation.

The IRR is designed as an objective measure of the rate of return actually earned by a project and may therefore be used as a device for comparing the merits of a series of competing projects.

This method suffers from a serious limitation which to a lesser degree applies to NPV. This limitation derives from the presumption that the cash generated by a project having a given IRR may be re-invested in additional opportunities which generate exactly the same IRR. If, on the assumption that a company presently earns income at a rate less than the IRR of a proposed research project, and if it has no alternative investment plans other than to undertake a selection of research projects having lower IRRs than this project, then there is manifestly no opportunity to re-invest at a rate equal to the IRR of that project. Hence, IRR is considered by many to be a meaningless or at least, severely restrictive concept. Nevertheless the method has a certain popularity, as although it is more suspect than NPV in respect of the above limitation, it does overcome the problem of defining the discount rate required for the NPV method.

8   Probabilistic appraisal techniques   The techniques considered so far are based on the assumption that management is able to provide accurate single-point estimates of the variables concerned. For instance, R&D costs, product unit costs and selling prices are assumed to have discrete values not open to question. In the nature of things, however, it is likely that functional management when requested to provide the necessary information for project appraisal, will not wish to commit themselves to hard and fast single-point estimates, but will prefer to define 'bands' within which the value of variable is likely to fluctuate and finally settle. For example, marketing management may suggest that the selling price of the product considered for development is between £2 and £5, with a most likely value of £3.

Given this type of information, techniques, usually computer based, are available to simulate the outcomes. They establish a probability distribution for each variable and, by a random sampling from each, use an iterative process to calculate the most probable result and the margin by which this is likely to vary. They may be extended to incorporate a facility for sensitivity analysis, which allows the significance of each variable to be examined independently. For instance, the expected completion data of a particular R&D project may be varied, whilst holding the other variables constant, to see the effect, if any, upon the overall profitability of that proposal. These simulative techniques may be applied to any of the measures already discussed to give, for example, a likely duration for the pay-back period, together with estimates of the shortest and longest durations.

In recent years, financial models have been developed using simulation methods, which enable management to appreciate the impact of a proposal on the short- and long-term profitability and liquidity of the company as a whole. After forecasting the existing business of the company, the new proposal may be superimposed upon those operations to predict the combined effect of both. Such methods should continue to play an increasing role in assisting management to appraise investment opportunities, and in particular should develop an enhanced ability to evaluate the risks to be accepted or rejected.

The overriding point to be made is that no-one technique is the panacea for appraising R&D proposals. Instead, management must be encouraged to use an appropriate selection to obtain a balanced and objective view of the comparative merits of opportunities available to them.

5.6 SELECTING THE OPTIMUM PORTFOLIO OF R&D PROJECTS

The next stage in the planning process is to select a portfolio of projects. Selection to date will have identified a series of projects which exhibit necessary strategic qualifications and which show some likelihood of contributing to corporate profits. The problem is to select a series of projects which are suitable for research and which together will satisfy the following conditions:

1   A balance in terms of research direction consistent with the objectives of the firm.
2   A balance in terms of:
    a   individual project risk;
    b   portfolio risk;
    c   overall risk to the company.
3   A high probability that some of the projects will make a sufficient contribution to profits to justify the costs of the R&D activity.
4   Full utilisation of the research department's technical skill and physical resources.
5   The aim of maximising long-term corporate profitability.

Simplified, the aim is to achieve a trade-off which will minimise risk and maximise financial return. Portfolio selection is a complex field, and one in which theoretical developments are not yet able to provide generally acceptable solutions. This is mainly because great difficulty is experienced in defining an *attitude* to risk which permits a decision as to whether a certain level of uncertainty is acceptable or not, although statistical probabilities can be used to assess the extent of project risk.

Despite this difficulty, much work has been done in devising solutions to the problem of resource allocation between competing projects. Techniques such as linear and dynamic programming can be used to search for that combination of projects, having different resource requirements, which will maximise expected profitability.

These techniques are also capable of handling one further problem of project selection; namely, project interdependency. In the event that the selection of one project affects the appeal of another, then this condition must be considered. It is suggested that for these effects to be properly analysed, individual projects should, in the first instance, be evaluated on the assumption that no interdependency exists. For example, if two separate projects require substantial investment in the same item of capital equipment, then this requirement should be incorporated in both the individual project appraisals. Suppose that one project is shown to be profitable and another loss-making, after including those capital requirements in both project evaluations. When searching for the most profitable portfolio, it may be found that by accommodating this feature ('doubling up'), the loss-making project will, by inclusion in the portfolio, make that portfolio more profitable than will the inclusion of a third profitable project, which does not require use of the capital equipment in question. This is a simple example, but it will be appreciated that the problem may become highly complex, when considering for instance, the likely sales mix of a number of products which may result from undertaking a particular portfolio of research projects.

It is beyond the scope of this book to examine these selection methods in detail because the problems they handle and the techniques are complex. A useful exposition, made by Carsberg [4], is recommended as a basic introduction.

5.7   CONCLUSION

This chapter illustrates the basic steps in planning the R&D programme, which are:
1   Review of current activities.
2   Screening of all possible research ideas.
3   Appraisal of 'candidate' proposals.
4   Selection of a portfolio of 'qualified' projects.

Appraisal and selection are vital aspects of this system, but without adequate review of current activities and proper screening of
research proposals, the resulting programme is likely to fall short of
that required to meet R&D, and ultimately corporate, objectives.

The planning system does not end with the selection of a portfolio of suitable projects. It must continue by stimulating the
operational planning, execution, and control of projects, so that the
expectations raised at the appraisal stage are satisfied by the ability
of the R&D function in particular and the company in general.

6 PRINCIPLES OF BUDGETARY CONTROL

6.1 LINKING COSTS AND ACHIEVEMENTS, AND THE FUNCTIONS OF BUDGETARY CONTROL

The principles of budgetary control are well established. Budgeting has been known for centuries, and budgetary control in the sense of pre-determining performances and costs for application in industry has been developed and applied since the early 1920s. Indeed standard costing and budgetary control emerged together from the needs of managers to know and understand the financial implications of what they were attempting to achieve.

Although budgetary control has existed for so long, there are many variations dependent upon the type of business, the management philosophy being pursued and the extent to which control is to be exercised over the individual parts of a business.

In addition to these differences, there are others that affect the operation of budgetary control as a means of planning and control. Establishing budgets implies having realistic performance and expense levels which are linked with the work to be done. Unfortunately, this linking of achievements and expenses is not always achieved, with the result that little or no control is exercised. In fact, all that happens is that managers are told how much they are committed to spend, but little or no attempt is made to relate this to the level of efficiency achieved.

With R&D, there is some difficulty in relating achievement with expenditure incurred. The uncertainty of the benefits to be obtained from R&D, may mean that any attempt to control within strict limits may nullify the programme. Yet unless some attempt is made to relate the expenditure to results achieved and at the same time to measure its impact upon the cash flow, there can be no realistic management of R&D and of a company as a whole.

Budgetary control links together a number of functions in a manner which allows the possible financial consequences to be determined and, subsequently, when the activities have been performed, it allows control to be exercised. These functions are summarised below.

1 Forecasting This is the pre-determination of likely events, generally in relation to a company's activities. The concern is with probabilities and, consequently, the statements resulting from the forecasts cannot be regarded as part of the budgetary control until considered in the light of corporate objectives, as well as existing and possible future constraints and other relevant issues.

2 Planning This function is concerned with deciding how the corporate objectives are to be achieved. In addition, it means consideration of alternative plans and selection of plans that optimise the results to be achieved. In this sense, to 'optimise' means:
a   earning an adequate return on capital employed (or other suitable measure) ;
b   achieving financial stability so that the company can continue to exist.

The second requirement is of vital importance when looking at R&D. As shown in the chapters which deal with the accounting for R&D, there may be considerable expenditure incurred in a particular year which does not relate to that year when calculating profit. If it is decided to carry forward this expenditure, the cash and profit will be 'out of balance'. There should always be reluctance to defer expenditure in this way, but where the accounting procedures followed represent a true and fair view and deferment is justified, the fact remains that the problem of imbalance will occur. Expenditure has been incurred and cash depleted, and, therefore, liquidity problems may exist, despite apparently profitable trading.

3 Organising This is the setting up of a structure which takes into account the relationships between departments and people as well as showing the relative responsibilities (see Chapter 3). This function

should also include participative management which requires managers to take an actual part in preparing their own budgets. This means
that the corporate objectives as specified by the board, are translated
into objectives of individual departments including R&D. Responsible
managers should be required to give their views and evaluate them in
financial terms. Subsequently these should be discussed by senior
managers and either approved or rejected. In the latter case, further
discussions would follow until an acceptable solution was found. The
managers should be concerned in establishing the budgets and should
understand the reasons why they have to be set at the levels finally
determined.

4   Coordinating   This is the process of drawing together all
functions and plans so that they work in harmony. With R&D there
could be a considerable overlap and waste, unless developments which
are taking place in one area are known and taken into account by
others. With large companies, a senior manager may have the task of
coordinating R&D and capital projects, so that their impact upon the
business as a whole can be appreciated and fully exploited.

5   Controlling   This is the function dealing with the achievement of
the plans made. As plans are carried out in an effort to achieve the
corporate objectives, there should be regular monitoring of results so
that any deviations from the limitations indicated in the plans can be
watched and, where appropriate, corrective action can be taken.

   In addition to the periodical control of expenditure, there would
also be the longer-term checks such as post-installation audits of R&D
projects. In this way it should be possible to see whether the research
function is providing long-term financial benefits.
   These five functions are integral parts of managing a business. What
therefore is required, is for a budgetary control system to be so designed that the functions can be carried out as a natural part of managing
R&D. An outline of how this may be achieved is now given.

6.2   R&D PROGRAMME BUDGET

For R&D to function correctly there should be an overall programme
to link long-term planning with the short-term budget. For example,
a company might have a ten-year plan for R&D broken down into ten
yearly budgets, each year representing the immediate priorities,
bearing in mind the constraints, including the cash available. The precise length of period for this long-term plan will depend upon the
business operations and although ten years is given as a guide, this

may be shorter or longer, depending upon circumstances.

The programme approach should consider the R&D corporate objectives. It should then show in broad terms what achievements are envisaged, together with expenditure to be incurred year-by-year. For the budget year, however, full details would be required.

6.2.1 The amount to spend

As a first step it will be necessary to determine how much can be spent on R&D. There are different ways of looking at this problem, the main alternatives being as follows.

1 On a technical estimate of the expenditure required to achieve a stated result   This means that a company is viewing R&D as having specific objectives which can be accomplished, providing sufficient money is spent. This approach might be logical for some types of business, but in others where the results are uncertain, there may be difficulty in assessing the volume of expenditure needed to produce a stated result. The very nature of R&D makes uncertainty an inevitable factor.

2 An amount based on how much a company can afford   This can be viewed in a number of ways; for example, on the basis of cash available for R&D or on how much should be spent in order to keep up with competitors. For many companies this second approach will be the one adopted. The precise amount may be determined by reference to some performance measure such as one of the following:
a   a percentage of total sales; or
b   a percentage based on profits earned; or
c   a similar amount to that spent by competitors.
The calculation may be based on last year's figures or on current budgeted figures. If the latter are realistic they may be used as the basis. All these measures allow the total sum permitted in a period to be stated with certainty. As will be appreciated, these methods do not necessarily measure the effectiveness of the R&D function, nor do they indicate whether too much or too little is being spent. For example, at a time when sales and profits are falling when figures are based on past results, R&D expenditure may have to be increased. Use of method *(a)* above, based on current budgeted sales would lead to a decision to curtail the activity. Yet this may be the time when new products are essential.

3 An amount based on assessment of a variety of relevant factors, such as the need for R&D, the effort required, the cash available, and the expected earnings from the function   This combined approach

may give the best results. It establishes how much a company should   83
spend, by taking account of all relevant factors in making the decision.
The expenditure level established will form the R&D budget for the
year and expenditure incurred will be subject to the discipline of budgetary control.

6.2.2   Establishing the immediate objectives

For budgetary control purposes it will be necessary to establish which
projects should appear in the forthcoming budget, and in this connection the following factors should be considered:

1   Relative priorities of the possible projects   This will depend on
the products and methods being developed and therefore there will be
a reference to the overall corporate plans, but more specifically to
other areas affected, such as marketing. For example, where it is clear
that a new product is required, priority might be given to the development of this item in preference to any other.

2   Existing facilities including staff, premises and equipment   Where
facilities are available for carrying out a particular line of investigation,
there may be a preference shown for projects that can conveniently be
fitted into the existing framework.

3   Availability of finance   Whilst the aim should be to have a reasonably stable R&D programme, consideration should be given to growth
of the activity when sufficient finance is available. If, owing to
increased cash flow from trading, or the sale of a factory, or other
fixed assets, cash becomes available in a particular year, then it may be
wise to programme heavy R&D expenditure in that period, particularly
if the future availability of finance is in doubt.
   A document for setting out the anticipated R&D expenditure over
a long period is shown in Figure 6.1. As indicated earlier, the concern
is with main items of expenditure. The authorisation of individual
projects would then have to be given attention as explained in the next
section.

6.3   PROJECT BUDGETS

The budgets for individual projects should be integrated into the overall
budgetary control system. They are usually in the form of a split budget
— part for costs in the nature of capital expenditure, and the remainder
as a conventional revenue expenditure budget.

ABC Enterprises Limited

Long-range (10 year) R&D expenditure programme (£'000)

	1973	1974	1975	1976	1977	1978	1979	1980	1981	1982
New product innovation:										
Materials	–	3	8	13	13	3	–	–	5	18
Labour	–	2	12	13	13	10	5	6	10	12
Overheads	–	5	30	34	34	27	10	14	30	35
	–	10	50	60	60	40	15	20	45	65
Capital equipment expenditure	–	15	25	5	5	–	–	–	5	15
	–	25	75	65	65	40	15	20	50	80
Existing product development:										
Materials	10	7	7	7	–	–	5	10	14	15
Labour	10	8	8	8	–	3	6	6	6	7
Overheads	25	20	20	20	–	7	14	14	15	18
	45	35	35	35	10	10	25	30	35	40
Capital equipment expenditure	20	10	–	–	–	–	5	10	15	–
	65	45	35	35	10	10	30	40	50	40
Total product innovation and development:										
Expense	45	45	85	95	60	50	40	50	80	105
Capital equipment	20	25	25	5	5	–	5	10	20	15
	65	70	110	100	65	50	45	60	100	120
New production processes:										
=										
=										
	15	20	20	10	5	30	50	70	30	10
Existing production processes:										
=										
=										
	20	17	13	20	20	20	30	20	20	20
TOTAL R&D ANNUAL BUDGET	100	107	143	130	90	100	125	150	150	150

Figure 6.1 R&D programme budget

The whole question of accounting for research and development should be considered in the light of accepted procedures for capital expenditure. The main question is whether the expenditure incurred results in benefits that accrue in the current or subsequent years. The most acceptable procedure is to write off R&D expenditure each year: this avoids deferring costs and showing them in the accounts as assets. If benefits will arise in future years and can be forecast with reasonable accuracy, then the amounts can be capitalised and written off against the anticipated revenue. This is an oversimplification, because many projects will not achieve benefits in the future and will have to be written off in the form of losses. However provided that the rules for distinguishing capital and revenue expenditure are followed consistently, and a reasonable amount is charged each year, no serious distortion should occur. As indicated, wherever possible, as a matter of financial prudence, accountants would prefer to write off R&D expenditure when incurred.

6.3.1 The interlocking budgetary control system

An appreciation of how the different budgets interlock into an overall financial control system can be seen by reference to Figure 6.2. It will be seen that budgets are required for all the major areas including R&D. Other budgets could be affected by what is included in the R&D budget, and the size of the latter can have a considerable influence on the other budgets. For example, a heavy R&D programme would have considerable influence on the cash budget. It would also affect purchase and capital expenditure budgets.

6.3.2 What is the R&D budget?

The R&D budget will be made up of that part of the programme earmarked as top priority for the budget period. It will consist of a number of R&D projects plus some general expenditure which cannot be allocated to specific projects. As a first requirement it is essential to draw up detailed budgets for the following:

1 *Main R&D projects with reference to their size, expected date of completion, expenditure required and other details*
2 *General budget for R&D expenditure not included in the project budgets*
3 *Manpower and staff budget to cover the requirements under (1) and (2).*
4 *A capital expenditure budget for fixed assets and other facilities*

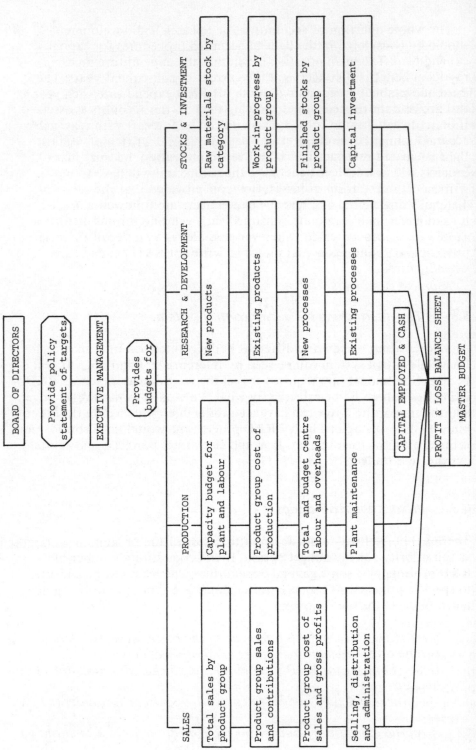

Figure 6.2 The budget framework

which are not consumed in the period in question.

5   *Cost budgets for material, labour and expense to be incurred in the budget period.*
6   *Cash budget for R&D.*

These budgets will be integrated into a total R&D budget and into total budgets for related activities such as capital expenditure, manpower and cash.

When looking at the R&D proposals as a whole, some consideration might be given to recovering part of the cost of selling some of the services to other companies. If this happens, then job cost sheets will be opened against which fees received from customers will be credited. There may also be scope for recovery of technical know-how provided to outsiders and in some cases from the use of patents and trade marks by licencees in this country and abroad.

The R and D budgets are now considered in the order indicated.

1   Main R&D projects with reference to their size, expected date of completion, expenditure required and other details   Each project to be included in the current year's operations should be evaluated by reference to the work required to carry out the stipulated objectives. The basis for the costs would be the R&D authorisation form discussed in Chapter 7. The total costs for each project, together with the gneeral costs, should be capable of being reconciled with the detailed cost budgets described later. From a control point of view, it is essential that an R&D project sheet should be used to record all expenditure to date, so that where overspending appears inevitable, supplementary authorisation can be obtained. In this way it will be possible to indicate how far a project has developed, what it has cost and how far the plans made have been achieved. With serious overspending, there should be a special investigation. A summary of projects may be presented in the form shown in Figure 6.3.

2   General budget for R&D expenditure not included in the project budgets   Where the general administrative costs cannot be allocated or apportioned to individual projects with any reasonable accuracy, there may be a case for preparing a separate budget to cover them. In effect, these are fixed costs which relate to the R&D function, and it can be argued that once the decision has been made to provide a given level of facilities and staff, then little can be done in a short period to control these costs. In other cases, the view may be taken that a fair proportion of these costs should be charged to individual projects, especially if there is a causal relationship between the cost and a specific project.

If fixed costs are kept separately, the statement given in Figure 6.4 may be appropriate.

ABC Enterprises Limited	Summary of research and development projects			Year: 1973
		Project A	Project B	Project C	Total
Project: Commencement date		1/1/72	1/1/73	31/3/73	
Planned completion date		30/6/74	31/12/76	30/6/75	
Expected completion date		31/7/74	31/12/76	30/6/75	
		£'000	£'000	£'000	£'000
Project: Total approved expenditure: revenue		110	50	45	205
capital		35	10	--	45
		145	60	45	250
Revenue costs: Prior year(s): Budget		30	--	--	30
Variance		(5)	--	--	(5)
Actual		35	--	--	35
Current year budget: Material		10	6	4	20
Labour		10	4	3	17
Overheads		25	10	8	43
		45	20	15	80
Future year(s) budget		35	30	30	95
TOTAL EXPECTED REVENUE COSTS		115	50	45	210
Capital costs: Prior year(s): Budget		5	--	--	5
Variance		-	--	--	-
Actual		5	--	--	5
Current year budget		20	--	--	20
Future year(s)		10	--	--	20
TOTAL EXPECTED CAPITAL COSTS		35	10	--	45
Project variances expected at completion:					
Revenue		(5)	--	--	(5)
Capital		--	--	--	--
TOTAL		(5)	--	--	(5)

Note: Unfavourable variances are in parentheses. If, after project review, costs for the current and/or future years are expected to exceed budget then this feature may be incorporated in the schedule and included under 'Project variances expected at completion'.

ABC Enterprises Limited	Research and Development Department fixed costs budget for year ending 31 December 1972			
Expense item	Budget for 1973, £	Actual expenses		Comments
		1972, £	1971, £	
Payroll:				
Salaries				
Research assistants (2)	2,500	1,200	1,100	Additional assistant from 1/1/73
Typists (1)	1,300	1,100	900	
NI	700	450	400	
Pensions	1,200	800	750	
	5,700	3,550	3,150	
Rent	4,500	3,500	3,500	Rent review due April 1973
Rates	1,750	1,650	1,500	
Stationery	950	800	850	
Depreciation of equipment	2,000	1,800	1,500	
Computer time	1,200	1,000	800	
Magazines and journals	150	100	100	
General expenses	350	400	300	Previously included staff advertising which is now personnel cost
TOTAL	16,600	12,800	11,700	

Figure 6.4 Budget of fixed costs for R&D

3 *Manpower and staff budget to cover the requirements under (1) and (2)*   In drawing up the manpower estimates and subsequently the budgets, reference will be made to how many staff will be required to carry out the work. Starting with the Director of Research, there would then be a breakdown into the various manpower categorie such as scientific or technical workers, administrative staff, laboratory assistants, and any general assistants required for maintaining the facilities. The various categories would be listed and expressed in financial terms, either in the fixed or detailed costs budgets, explained in a later section.

4 *A capital expenditure budget for fixed assets and other facilities which are not consumed in the period in question*   If a company decides to make its own plant and machinery, testing equipment or otl fixed assets, the normal procedures for authorising capital expenditure should be followed. This will require a capital expenditure authorisation form which gives the details and the justification for the expenditure. A job cost sheet will be opened on which to charge the costs and against which control can be exercised as the job proceeds. When the fixed asset is completed, this would then become a part of the capital employed and would be classified on the balance sheet under the appropriate heading such as 'Plant and Machinery'. The appropriate amount of depreciation would be charged each year.

Although there is great similarity between capital expenditure and R&D expenditure which is not written off in the year it is incurred, a clear distinction should be made between these two classes of expense. With capital expenditure there is usually a fixed asset which could possibly be sold on the open market. On the other hand, any R& expenditure which is deferred in a particular year is more in the nature of a fictitious asset which should be kept separate. Where possible, R& costs should be charged to the year in question, thus avoiding the problems of capitalisation.

What should be appreciated is that R&D machinery and equipment can present special problems which are not present for capital expenditure for the production function. In turn, these may call for separate treatment of the fixed assets. In this connection relevant considerations are as follows (many of these points are discussed in [5]):

a *Obsolescence*   Because of the uncertainty of R&D work, the life of fixed assets may be relatively short. Accordingly, a decision should be made on whether an accelerated rate of depreciation should be used, thus writing off total costs within the estimated life.

b *Special-purpose equipment*   Where equipment is made or purcha ed to carry out a highly specialised role, it probably means that

the useful life is linked with the R&D project. If the latter is
abandoned, or there is a change in approach, the cost of expensive equipment may become chargeable to that project simply
because there is no alternative use. In the interests of developing
a sound accounting policy, it may be better to classify special-
purpose equipment from the start and write it off within a short
period.

c *Excessive or harsh usage*   Equipment for normal production
purposes will generally be utilised at a set rate which enables an
economical life to be achieved. However, with research equipment the main purpose may be to test it out under the most
difficult conditions with resultant wear and tear, and even des-
truction. Often modifications and adaptations are made which
also accelerate the wearing out of the equipment. It will be
appreciated that when dealing with new projects suitable equipment may not be available and for this reason the normal rules
for capital and revenue cannot always apply.

From these observations it should be apparent that whilst the normal accounting rules for distinguishing capital and revenue should be
applied there is difficulty in applying them rigidly. Where the obsolescence factor is quite high, a more rapid write off of equipment should
be recommended. There should be a flexible approach but, at the
same time, the policy pursued should allow consistency to be achieved.
Depreciation charges should reflect a realistic assessment of the useful
life of the equipment after considering all relevant factors.

5   Cost budgets for material, labour and expense to be incurred in the
budget period   Under this heading would appear all the revenue
expenditure to be incurred within the R&D area. Where fixed expenses
are to be kept separate, these would be included on a separate budget
as indicated earlier.

The precise lay-out and content of these budgets would suffice to
show the three classes of expenditure. With a complex organisation
there would be separate budgets to cover labour, materials and overhead, and these would possibly be backed up by detailed schedules
showing the expenditure to be allowed in the particular budget period.
Where the work is to be phased the budgets may be broken down to
show the time of year when the expenditure is to be incurred. It will
be usual to have a monthly or quarterly control period for each budget, thus allowing comparisons to be made between actual expenditure
and budgeted allowances.

6   Cash budget for R&D   Research expenditure can be substantial,
and should be covered in a cash budget. For planning and control

purposes it is essential to have a detailed breakdown of expenditure expected to be incurred. With a possible shortage of cash; action should be taken to schedule the R&D expenditure for a different period or, where there is a commitment, to ensure that cash is made available from alternative sources.

This linking of the cash requirements with the R&D function is one of the most neglected areas of accountancy. There is a mistaken belief that if a company is earning a profit then the cash needs should be covered automatically. This erroneous belief has led many companies into difficulties and this coordination between the cash and cost budgets should be given top priority.

6.4   ACCOMPLISHING THE MANAGEMENT FUNCTIONS

Reference has been made to the functions of planning, coordination and control. In preparing the budgets, these important functions must be kept in mind.

The budgets represent plans that are intended to achieve the corporate objectives. Accordingly, in looking at them for a future budget period, formal and informal discussions should take place among the managers concerned. In addition, the budget controller, who would possibly be the management accountant, would coordinate the necessary work through his own department.

The method by which coordination is achieved depends upon the size of the company and the circumstances. Some companies can manage with no formal organisation structure, such as an R&D budget committee, but others find the latter essential. Accordingly, no hard and fast rules can be laid down as to how the objectives can be realised. Research and practice have indicated that much misunderstanding can be eliminated, and better results obtained when managers actively participate in the preparation of the budgets, and understand how they can implement them.

The subject of organisation is covered in Chapter 3. At this stage, however, it is relevant to establish an organisation structure that relates to committees and procedures used by a company for examining the R&D function, both at the planning and control stages.

6.5   CONTROL OF R&D EXPENDITURE

There are various stages at which control should be exercised, either when looking at performance or when comparing budgeted allowances with actual costs. Detailed consideration of post-audit procedures is given in Chapter 9. In this section the concern is with looking at the budgeted costs.

If budgetary control is to be taken to its logical conclusion, then it is necessary to produce variances which are analysed to determine why they have occurred. There are different ways of attempting control which are as follows:

1 Reporting variances for each project (a fair proportion of fixed costs having been charged to individual projects):
   a in total;
   b by type of expense.
2 Reporting variances in total for the whole R&D organisation:
   a against projects, isolating any significant deviations on specific projects;
   b against general administration costs (not allocated to projects), indicating any extraordinary expenditure.

An alternative classification is to look at variances under the following headings:
1 Basic research.
2 Applied research.
3 Development work separating:
   a products;
   b methods;
   c technical know-how.
4 New ideas and developments which are covered by a contingency fund where the business is of the type where new ideas have to be exploited quickly.

For control purposes it is usually advisable to separate research from development work. In practice there may be separate departments dealing with these two functions, which would be treated as separate budget centres.

The individual projects are usually regarded as the lowest control point for the purpose of assessing whether or not plans have been achieved. This is in accordance with responsibility accounting principles where, for cost control, it is recognised that reference should be made to those individuals who actually incur expenditure. However, with a function such as R&D, there should be constant reference to the results being achieved as well as the related costs.

6.6 OPERATING STATEMENTS FOR R&D

In presenting information to management it is necessary to design appropriate forms which show the plans made, the achievements accomplished, and the variances which occur from one control period to

ABC Enterprises Ltd	RESEARCH AND DEVELOPMENT OPERATING STATEMENT	Period No. 9 Ended: 30/9/--

This period			Expenditure	Year to date		
Budget £	Actual £	Var. £		Budget £	Actual £	Var. £
			ALLOCATED EXPENSE: Basic research:			
			Project A or Material			
			Project B Labour			
			Project C Overhead			
950	1010	(60)		8500	7900	600
			Applied research:			
			Project D or Material			
			Project E Labour			
			Project F Overhead			
1750	1700	50		12150	14425	(2275)
			Development:			
			Project G or Material			
			Project H Labour			
			Project J Overhead			
1950	1975	(25)		17350	17465	(115)
			Special innovation work: Details			
-	-	-		-	-	-
-	-	-		-	-	-
4650	4685	(35)	TOTAL PROJECT EXPENSE	38000	39790	(1790)
			NON-ALLOCATED EXPENSE: Payroll:			
475	495	(20)	Salaries	4275	4450	(175)
60	64	(4)	National insurance	525	550	(25)
100	100	-	Pensions	900	920	(20)
365	365	-	Rent	3300	3300	-
145	145	-	Rates	1300	1300	-
80	45	35	Stationery	700	675	25
167	175	(8)	Depreciation	1500	1450	50
100	160	(60)	Computer time	900	1050	(150)
10	7	3	Magazines and journals	100	95	5
30	47	(17)	General expenses	270	305	(35)
1532	1603	(71)	TOTAL NON-ALLOCATED EXPENSE	13770	14095	(325)
6182	6288	(106)	TOTAL R&D ACTIVITY	51770	53885	(2115)

Figure 6.5 R&D operating statement - 1 (unfavourable variances are in parentheses

ABC Enterprises Ltd			RESEARCH AND DEVELOPMENT OPERATING STATEMENT	Period No. 9 Ended: 30/9/--		
This period			Expenditure	Year to date		
Budget £	Actual £	Var. £		Budget £	Actual £	Var. £
			ALLOCATED EXPENSE:			
			Major projects:			
1500	1430	70	X	10000	12150	(2150)
950	1010	(60)	Y	8500	7900	600
1700	1710	(10)	Z	15200	15190	10
4150	4150	-		33700	35240	(1540)
500	535	(35)	TOTAL MINOR PROJECTS	4300	4550	(250)
4650	4685	(35)	TOTAL PROJECT EXPENSE	38000	39790	(1790)
			NON-ALLOCATED EXPENSE:			
			Payroll:			
475	495	(20)	Salaries	4275	4450	(175)
60	64	(4)	National Insurance	525	550	(25)
100	100	-	Pensions	900	920	(20)
365	365	-	Rent	3300	3300	-
145	145	-	Rates	1300	1300	-
80	45	35	Stationery	700	675	25
167	175	(8)	Depreciation	1500	1450	50
100	160	(60)	Computer time	900	1050	(150)
10	7	3	Magazines and journals	100	95	5
30	47	(17)	General expenses	270	305	(35)
1532	1603	(71)	TOTAL NON-ALLOCATED EXPENSE	13770	14095	(325)
6182	6288	(106)	TOTAL R&D ACTIVITY	51770	53885	(2115)

VARIANCES

(106)	UNDER/(OVER)SPENDING	(2115)
-	BUDGET REVISION	-
(106)	TOTAL VARIANCES	(2115)

Figure 6.6 R&D operating statement - 2 (unfavourable variances in parentheses)

another. These then provide the basis for management action and for ensuring that R&D is kept within reasonable limits.

Because of the varied nature of R&D, it is impossible to generalise on what should be regarded as a significant variance. There are those who state catagorically that to attempt to control R&D expenditure is a fruitless task, which only frustrates research workers. Although a certain amount of freedom of action is essential, it should be possible to work within the constraints imposed by properly constructed budgets.

Within each company it will be necessary to lay down procedures for authorising expenditure and subsequently for controlling within the margins defined by signficant variances. Thus a company may decide that a deviation of 5 per cent on labour costs would call for an investigation and a report from the manager concerned. What is really required is anticipation on the part of the managers to ensure that any additional expenditure is covered in budgets and no excessive overrun is allowed. This is not just a question of extra cost, but also of the provision of additional cash which may be in short supply.

Examples of operating statements are given in Figures 6.5 and 6.6.

7
CONTROLLING THE R&D PROGRAMME

Once the programme of future R&D is planned and approved, the necessary control must be organised to ensure that progress is achieved according to plan. This chapter deals with the authorisation of expenditure and also serves to outline the techniques and review procedures employed in controlling a programme.

7.1 AUTHORISATION OF R&D EXPENDITURE

It was stressed in the previous chapter that budgetary control is far from being a system which merely stipulates the maximum expenditure that a departmental manager may spend. Rather it is used to assist management to achieve the desired plans in the most efficient manner practicable. If this means using more resources than was originally thought necessary, the system will accommodate this factor, but its prime function is to highlight those areas where departures from the original plan have taken place. Moreover, the reasons for the deviations should be determined and prompt action taken.

Authorisation of expenditure is no more than an adjunct or corollary of an authorised plan, and should be regarded as such, but this view should not detract from the importance of controlling expenditure within the limits that a company can afford.

The act of authorisation will normally consist of issuing a project order. This in effect releases the project from 'cold storage' and empowers research personnel to charge their productive time, materials, and expenses to the project cost account. The order will preferably be of a format similar to that used for building up the cost estimate used for the project appraisal (see Figure 7.1).The schedule is designed on the basis of linking forecast costs directly with the programmed activities of the research project. Thus the costs of each activity may be related easily, via the activity numbers, to the scheduled activities identified on the bar charts and/or networks used for controlling progress of the project (see Sections 7.2.1 and 7.2.2).

The costs are allocated and apportioned to specific time periods in a manner which reflects the ability of research personnel to forecast likely progress. Usually, research costs relating to future periods cannot be predicted with accuracy, as long-term progress is dependent upon the outcome of short-term activity. Therefore the costs of, say, the first year of a project could be allocated or apportioned over each quarter (and sometimes over each month), whilst those of subsequent years' would be grouped initially in half-yearly or annual totals.

On the authority of the project order, costs incurred will be charged against the project. In order that the costs attributable to each project can be collected, it will be necessary to use a suitable form of coding system by which primary cost documentation can be referenced to individual projects. The type of system will vary according to the needs of the individual company, but it is likely to require the facility to identify some or all of the following features:

1   The type of research, for example,
    a   basic;
    b   applied;
    c   development; or
    d   new product;
    e   existing product;
    f   new production process;
    g   existing production process.
2   The customer or company-user department requesting the research project.
3   The individual project number.
4   The cost centre incurring the expense.
5   The activity number.

Expenditure authorisation for a project will not necessarily be a once and for all exercise. If research effort is required over and above the original estimate, then supplementary authorisation may be required. This eventuality was considered in the previous chapter and

Project reference no.	Start date: Finish date:	Project description:	Customer/user dept.:

Activity reference

Activity reference				Cost estimates, £							
Project phase	Activity number	Activity description	Cost head	Year 1 First qtr	Year 1 Second qtr	Year 1 Third qtr	Year 1 Fourth qtr	Year 2 First half	Year 2 Second half	Year 3	Year 4
I	1 – 2	Procure and explode competitor's product	Material	200							
			D/labour	80							
			Overhead	200							
				480							
	2 – 3	Produce drawings & complete technical specification	Material		50						
			D/labour		400						
			Overhead		1,000						
					1,450						
	3 – 6	Analyse and test sub-assembly AB12	Material		800						
			D/labour		300						
			Overhead		750						
					1,850						
			Plant		450						
					2,300						
	Etc.	Etc.				4,000	5,500				
II	20 – 21	Manufacture prototype	Material					2,000	1,400		
			D/labour					5,000	4,500		
			Overhead					12,500	11,250		
								19,500	17,150		
			Plant						1,550		
								19,500	18,700		
III IV	Etc.	Etc.								45,000	25,000
TOTAL REVENUE EXPENDITURE			114,430	480	3,300	3,000	4,000	19,500	17,150	42,000	25,000
TOTAL CAPITAL EXPENDITURE			7,500	–	450	1,000	1,500	–	1,550	3,000	–
TOTAL PROJECT COST			121,930	480	3,750	4,000	5,500	19,500	18,700	45,000	25,000

Authorisation date: Revision approval dates:

Figure 7.1 Authorised schedule of R&D project costs

should it occur it will be necessary to amend the 'Authorised Schedule of R&D Project Costs' to incorporate the revised estimates of resource consumption. Budgeted cost figures shown on the project operating statement will also be amended so that actual costs may be compared. Variances will be analysed in the normal way and those attributable to budget revisions separately identified.

7.2   TECHNIQUES FOR CONTROLLING THE R&D PROGRAMME

For the accountant and R&D manager, budgetary control is a vital aspect of project control. The primary function of the project executive is to control the resources available to him, and to achieve specified results. His work is essentially within the constraint of a certain supply of resources whose consumption may be monitored by the budgetary control system, but a control mechanism is also required with which to monitor both achievement and failure along the path of the research project.

It is vital that these two control mechanisms are inter-related and that progress reports generated by each, are integrated. Unless this is done regularly, there is a danger that any divergence from plan in terms of *physical* progress, will not be reconciled with its financial counterpart, or vice versa.

The techniques available for the control of projects are similar to those used for *operational* planning. A detailed project plan is devised in order to schedule the activities required for the achievement of the project goal, and, once this is prepared, control is obtained by ensuring that resources are used in accordance with the plan. Unless divergence from plan is experienced during the control phase, the overall project goal should be achieved.

There are basically two groups of planning and control techniques:

1   Those primarily concerned with the 'time scheduling' of project activities, and which are not extensively used to handle problems of resource allocation or usage — these include 'bar' or Gantt charts.
2   Those which incorporate time scheduling, and which concentrate attention on resource allocation and utilisation. They include the Programme Evaluation Review Technique (PERT) and the Critical Path Method (CPM).

A third method, Planning, Programming, Budgeting System (PPBS), which amounts to a fully integrated planning and control system, will also be discussed.

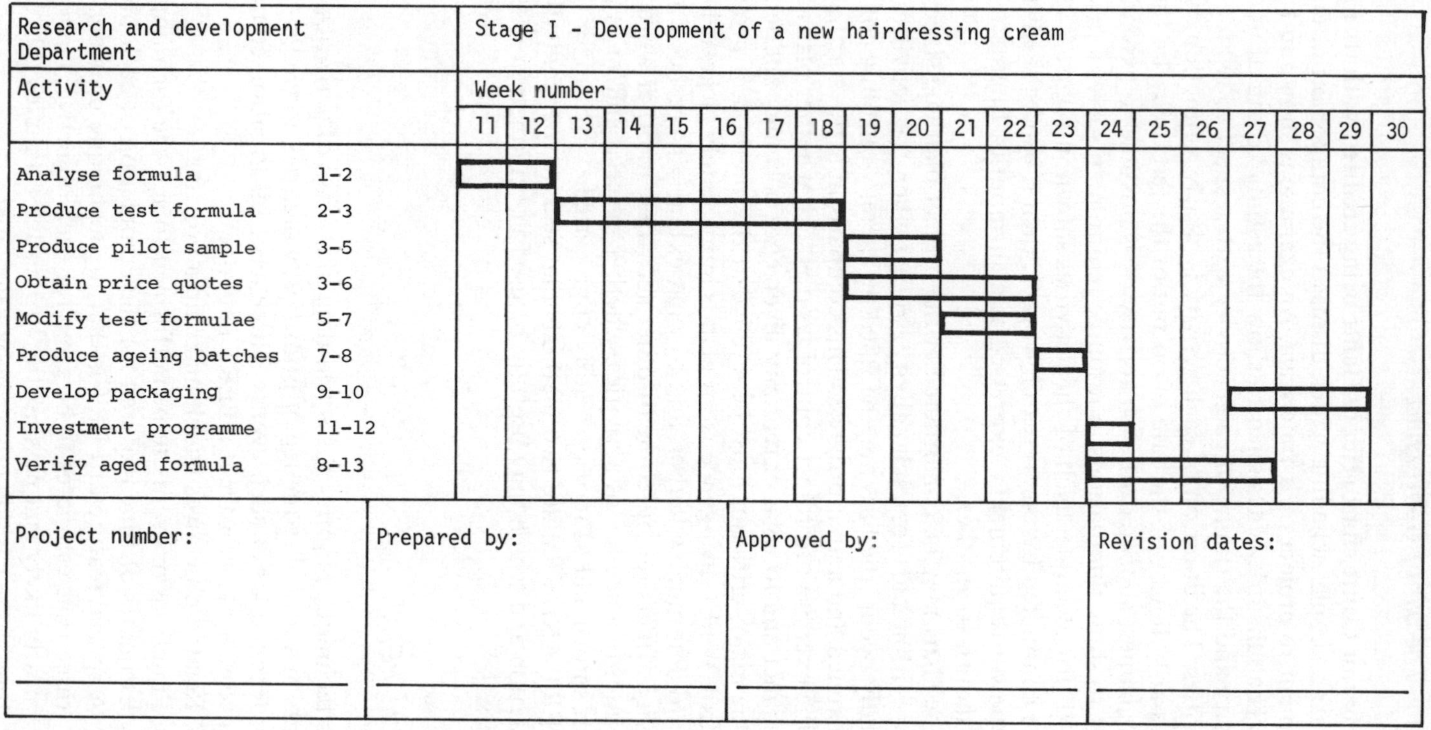

Research and development Department

Stage I – Development of a new hairdressing cream

Week number: 11 12 13 14 15 16 17 18 19 20 21 22 23 24 25 26 27 28 29 30

Activity	
Analyse formula	1-2
Produce test formula	2-3
Produce pilot sample	3-5
Obtain price quotes	3-6
Modify test formulae	5-7
Produce ageing batches	7-8
Develop packaging	9-10
Investment programme	11-12
Verify aged formula	8-13

Prepared by:

Approved by:

Revision dates:

Project number:

Figure 7.2 Bar or Gantt chart

The bar or Gantt chart (Henry Gantt being credited with its invention),is a simple schedule which displays the component operations of an entire project on a time scale. An example is shown in Figure 7.2. The schedule is designed to show the estimated duration of each activity and the timing of each activity with respect to related activities. The duration of each activity is clearly a function, not necessarily linear, of the rate of output of the resources, be they men or machines, allocated to each activity. It is possible to extend the chart to show fluctuations in resource requirements over a project's life. If, for example, each of the activities shown in Figure 7.2 is to be conducted by one research worker, then it can be seen that manpower requirements, expressed as man/months, fluctuate from one month to another.

The chart may be constructed at the project planning stage to show outline bars for each activity, so that when the activities actually occur, the bars may be filled in, thereby enabling comparison of planned and actual progress. This comparison is the starting point for the exercise of project control, as it is seen whether plans are being met and to what extent any divergence is being experienced.

One major criticism must be levelled at this method of project control. Whilst divergence from plan is immediately clear, it is not easy to determine whether, and to what extent, divergence on one activity affects the outcome of other activities. In other words, the full interdependency of activities, whether in series and/or in parallel, is not shown and cannot be readily appreciated.

PERT AND CPM are two methods that seek to overcome this limitation and which may usefully be used in conjunction with bar charts.

7.2.2   PERT

This technique requires the scheduling of a series of activities or events in a logical sequence of priorities, which acknowledges the interdependence of such events. Three basic information components are necessary to construct a PERT network:

1   Related objectives which make up a project.
2   Functions or events to be performed to achieve each objective.
3   Estimates of time required for the completion of each objective. A special feature of PERT is that the technique provides for three time estimates to be given for each objective, i.e. optimistic, mostly likely and pessimistic. From such estimates the 'expected time' for each objective can be calculated.

The network of activities or events is built up according to their various sequences and the result gives an entire plan of events; for example, to build a new vehicle or produce a new material. From the total network system a 'critical path' is identified. This path is derived from calculations of the cumulative times of sequenced events of the various network paths up to the point of project completion. The path is one which, from start to finish, requires the greatest cumulative expected time. An example given later in this chapter illustrates the concept of a network and identification of the critical path. Any time lost on events along the critical path will result in an increase in the total time taken to complete the project. Conversely, any time reduced or saved would have the opposite result. In the latter case, the whole course of the critical path may alter owing to savings in time achieved on the original critical path.

From a planning viewpoint, the advantages of constructing a network can be summarised as:

1   The formulation of the network in itself forces detailed analysis in content and depth that would otherwise, perhaps, not be carried out. The result is a programme that can be relied upon with greater certainty and one that is capable of closer control.

2   Once the network has highlighted the critical path and identified the 'slack' associated with non-critical paths, it is possible to re-appraise the resources available for each activity in order to achieve savings in time and costs. In addition, a major advantage accrues by being able to ignore delays in the progress of each non-critical activity by the amount of 'float' time available for the ensuing event; namely, the completion of that activity or of the following activity. The 'float' or 'slack' time is found by comparisons of the earliest and latest starting times of any activity. The latest time is arrived at by determining the times of activities and working backwards from the project completion date — the earliest time by working forward from the commencement date.

From a control viewpoint, after the scheduling stage and network completion, the task is simple. To achieve each activity in the plan for an R&D project, it is necessary to assign:

1   A time (usually expressed in weeks or days).
2   Technical man hours required (resource).

If there is an adequate system of accounting and reporting, which includes records of the actual time taken and the man hours used for each activity on completion, comparison of actual and planned results at each activity or event stage, allows for the control of time and costs throughout the duration of the project. The re-assessment of 'expected' times for activities throughout the duration of the project allows for a rapid re-appraisal of the project from which new critical paths may emerge. Given the constraint of completing a project by a given time, the re-assessment of times and resources required by various activities, provides management with a practical planning and control tool.

In addition to its use in controlling R&D projects, PERT has particular use in the formulation of the R&D budget programme. An R&D department will most probably have a given level of personnel and thereby technical man hours available, which, barring wild fluctuations, will form the basis of the R&D budget. Applied and development projects will be initially sequenced in order of priorities for inclusion in the budget year. These must be executed from the available manpower resources and, therefore, will compete with one another for the total number of technical manhours available. Sequential analysis of project activities in the depth required for PERT networks, enables a realistic assessment to be made of the man hours required for individual projects, and in aggregate. This assessment will then facilitate the selection of projects for inclusion in the budget. PERT can be of particular use in the development of the budget for:

1   Applied projects; that is, those specifically identified and capable of being assigned resources and completion dates.
2   Development projects, i.e. agreed areas of development but where the final product is not yet capable of specific identification. In these cases a PERT network can be evolved in less detail than for applied projects.

The final budget should be more precise than that obtained by less analytical methods and should stimulate the necessary commitment of R&D executives to their control function.

7.2.3 Example

To illustrate the above concept, assume the following project position shown in Table 7.1. Each event is designated by a circle in the network. The meaning of the figures in the various segments are as shown in Figure 7.3. The result of the network is a detailed integrated plan of the R&D department's activity in the creation and market launch of a new product.

It can be seen from the network diagram for this illustration (see Figure 7.4) that the critical path, indicated by the heavy trace, follows

TABLE 7.1

APPLIED PROJECT NO. 19	BUDGET YEAR 1974/75
Project title	Create new hairdressing cream compatible with that of competitor XYZ
Allowed project time	30 weeks
Period of project	Weeks 11–41
Project budget	£5000 revenue cost; £1500 capital; 760 technical man-hours

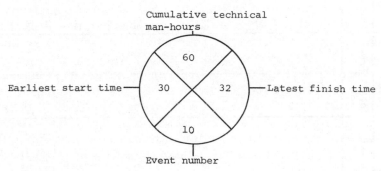

Figure 7.3

activities 1, 2, 3, 5, 7, 8, 13, 16, 17, 18, 19 and 20. This path follows that sequence of events having the maximum total duration, i.e. 30 weeks, as opposed to the sub-critical paths having total durations of 25 and 28 weeks, respectively.

The benefits of the PERT network compared with a conventional checklist method, see Table 7.2, which would entail the listing of activities only, not necessarily in logical sequence, may be:

1   A positive commitment by various managers to a well thought out plan which is seen to be achievable.
2   A planned launch date, can be aimed for with more confidence which may be vital owing to anticipated competitive actions or seasonal factors.
3   Diversion of effort to non-critical factors is avoided. Consider the position where the time, say, for obtaining capital equipment (activity numbers 12 - 16) is seven weeks instead of five as originally programmed. The PERT network indicates a total float of four weeks on the path 3-6-11-12-16. Providing the other events have been achieved on programme, the lengthened period of seven weeks to acquire the capital equipment can be

TABLE 7.2 Project activity schedule for network diagram

PROJECT TITLE: New hairdressing cream comparable with competitor's product XYZ

R&D Project Manager:
New Product Manager:

Target product launch date:
Project No.:   Budget:

Activity description	Activity number	Planned duration		Start		Float		Finish		Responsibility
		Weeks	Technical man-hours	Earliest	Latest	Total	Free	Earliest	Latest	
STAGE 1										
Analyse formula of competitor's product	1 – 2	2	80	11	11	0	0	13	13	
Produce own test formula with three levels of gel density & perfume levels	2 – 3	6	180	13	13	0	0	19	19	
Produce pilot samples of 1000 of each formula for test market ing in unidentified packaging	3 – 5	2	80	19	19	0	0	21	21	
Obtain price quotations & supplies availability for raw and packing materials at various quantity levels	3 – 6	4	40	19	19	4	0	23	27	
Modify test formulae as a result of test reports	5 – 7	2	80	21	21	0	0	23	23	
Produce batches for ageing tests	7 – 8	1	40	23	23	0	0	24	24	
Develop product and advertising concepts	5 – 9	6	Non R&D	21	21	2	0	27	29	
Develop packaging design	9 – 10	3	60	27	29	2	0	30	32	

Activity		Duration	R&D man-hours						
Calculate product costs & set initial selling prices – verify profitability of product	6 – 11	1	Non R&D	23	27	4	0	24	28
Determine capital investment programme	11 – 12	1	20	24	28	4	0	25	29
Verify aged formula for gel consistency and perfume retention	8 – 13	4	40	24	24	0	0	28	28
Check legal position and file initial patents & trademark	10 – 14	3	Non R&D	30	32	4	0	33	37
Prepare marketing plan & obtain authorisation for commercial production and launch	10 – 15	8	Non R&D	30	32	2	0	38	40
STAGE 2									
Obtain initial quantities of raw and packing materials	13 – 16	6	Non R&D	28	28	0	0	34	34
Order initial capital equipment	12 – 16	5	Non R&D	25	29	4	0	30	34
Produce pilot batch & run test shipment for breakages an appearance	16 – 17	2	40	34	34	0	0	36	36
Modify outer shippers to overcome breakages	17 – 18	1	40	36	36	0	0	37	37
Produce initial commercial quantities for launch programme	18 – 19	2	40	37	37	0	0	39	39
Launch ad. campaign	15 – 20	1	Non-R&D	38	40	2	0	39	41
Product distribution	19 – 20	2	20	39	39	0	0	41	41

TOTAL MANPOWER RESOURCE REQUIREMENT   760 technical man-hours

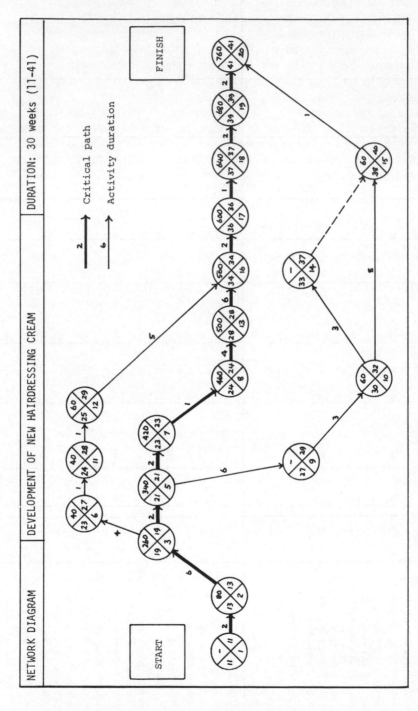

Figure 7.4 Network diagram for the development of a new hairdressing cream

accepted without affecting the final project completion date, i.e.
week 41. The decision required, if working from a conventional
checklist programme, might put back the product launch date,
or to pay an increased cost to obtain equipment elsewhere.
Under the PERT network, the precise position may be determined. In this example it is clear that the benefits of avoiding
unnecessary delay in the product launch date could be considerable, though not necessarily quantifiable, particularly if early
market penetration is the key to long-term consumer accpetance.
PERT is not a panacea for the R&D executive, but the illustration serves to show the advantages of detailed scheduling for the
planning and control of an R&D applied project.

7.2.4   Critical path analysis

The critical path method is similar to PERT, and many of the terms
are interchangeable. Basically, the difference lies in the time estimates for achieving each event. Under PERT each event is given three
time estimates for completion, from which a statistical, single 'expected time' is derived. Under CPM it is usual to assign a single time
for each event. After this stage PERT and CPM are, for all practical
purposes, identical.

   The advantages of a network analysis are that once the critical path
has been established, managers may consider, on a cost-benefit basis,
the merits of allocating such additional resources as would reduce the
overall project completion time. In this example, if it is possible to
increase sales by 20 per cent in the first year, by bringing the launch
date forward by two weeks, then perhaps it might be worth devoting
more technical manhours on say activity 2 - 3 to reduce elapsed time
for this activity, from six to four weeks.

7.2.5   Computer applications

Network analysis is ideally suited to a computer application. (A useful introductory text describing the use of network analysis for
project control is given in [6].) Many standard program packages are
available which reduce the initial complexity and 'set up' costs of
such a program to a minimum level. As already stated, PERT networks deal with time and resource allocation. The types of system
that may be utilised fall into four main categories:

1   Systems that deal only in time, that is between each event.
2   Systems that analyse costs but do not alter the time-based
    network.

3 Systems that analyse costs and adjust networks to optimise
time and costs.
4 Systems that consider resource availability, i.e. technical man-
hours in conjunction with costs, and produce cost networks
within present resource limitations.

7.2.6 PPBS

PPBS or Planning, Programming, Budgeting System is a technique of
planning and control development in the USA and which has achieved
much prominence since its successful application during the early
1960s, in the US Department of Defense. Since then, the technique
has been extensively applied to the resource allocation problems of
North American industry, as well as federal, and state government. It
has yet to attain equal popularity in Great Britain.

PPBS is an output-orientated technique which includes a detailed
analysis of the objectives, priorities and resource requirements of an
organisation and/or operation, in an attempt to maximise output in a
manner consistent with its objectives and constraints. It is beyond the
scope of this book to discuss PPBS in detail, but the following brief
description will serve to provide an outline. Readers interested in
pursuing the subject are referred to text by Rose [7], Novick [8]
and Marshall [9] for useful expositions.

1 What does PPBS mean?   The following are brief descriptions of
the terms Planning, Programming, Budgeting and Systems:
a   *Planning:* begins with the establishment of a set of measurable
objectives. These objectives are systematically determined and
reviewed in the light of experience of what appear to be
possible, and what is found to be practicable.
b   *Programming:* the process by which activities related to the
operation are formally scheduled or organised with respect to
the declared objectives. It includes detailed analysis and selection of alternative strategies, designed to produce an integrated
programme and financial plan for, say, the next five years.
c   *Budgeting:* the expansion of the first year of the programme
and financial plan into a working document which specifies in
detail, performance, expenditure and revenue targets for that
year.
d   *System:* that aspect of the technique which produces the information necessary at each stage of the PPBS process. It includes
not only the facility for comparing actual performance against
budget, but also the mechanism by which information is collected, collated, and disseminated throughout the entire objective setting, programming and budgeting operation.

The system is represented in Figure 7.5. The main components —
planning, programming, and budgeting are inter-linked one with
another by information flows — the systems feature of PPBS.

2 Advantages and disadvantages of PPBS The following are the
major criticisms levelled at *traditional* budgeting systems for planning
and controlling activities such as R&D.

a   The tendency for budgets to be based on the inputs to departments or sub-divisions of departments, rather than on outputs
related to their functional objectives.
b   The myopic influence of annual budgets covering projects of
multi-year duration.
c   The lack of recognition that projects are often mutually dependent.

PPBS was developed in an attempt to overcome these deficiencies,
and is characterised by the following main features:

a   Objectives are explicitly stated at the outset and activity programmes are structured with respect to the desired outputs.
b   The programme and financial plan are designed to cover a
number of years, usually dictated by the nature of the activity.
c   Continuous assessment is made of current activities and of the
availability of alternatives better suited to achieving the desired
objective(s).

PPBS embraces the principles of budgeting in an integrated scheme
of planning and programming, and is designed to overcome the
limitations inherent in budgetary control methods which, *when
operated without explicit reference to corporate objectives, planning
and control,* give rise to the criticisms cited above.
    PPBS is therefore analogous to an integrated system of corporate
objective setting, planning, organisation and control, in that it tailors
the principles applicable to the company as a whole, to the particular
needs of an operation whose aim is to maximise desirable output in
conditions of resource scarcity.
    It is said that this method is not new but merely represents an
intuitively obvious integration of planning and control techniques
which are already in wide use. Nevertheless, experience in the USA
provides evidence that the technique may be used successfully in the
planning and control of an operation in its entirety, with respect to
allied operations and with constant reference to declared objectives
and available resources.

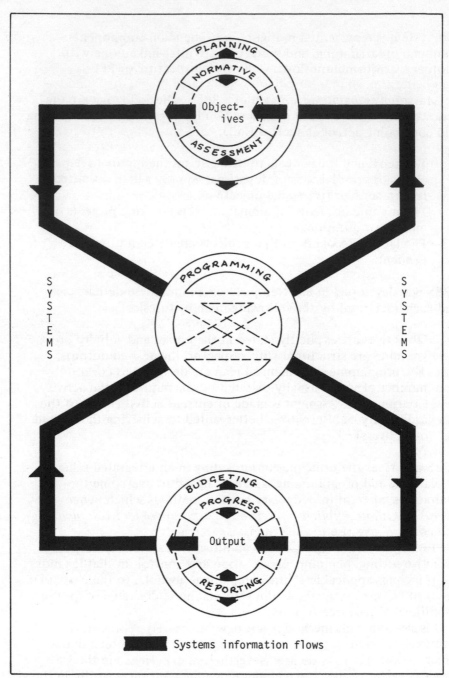

Figure 7.5   Schematic representation of PPBS

In putting the techniques discussed into perspective — PPBS, rather than being a technique for planning and controlling individual projects, as are PERT and CPM, is suitable for application to complete operations such as an R&D department. PERT and CPM may be usefully employed in conjunction with bar of Gantt charts to form a comprehensive project planning and control package. If satisfactory control is to be achieved over both the physical and financial facets of an R&D programme, then it is essential for the techniques outlined to be integrated into a system of budgetary control.

7.3 PROJECT REVIEW

Significant projects should be reviewed at corporate level to ensure that priorities are assessed at this, as well as at functional level. Regular checks should be made on the progress of projects to assess whether the results, time taken and costs are in accordance with plans. This process will determine the action required in the company's best interest, in view of the results obtained at the time of the check. Action may be required to bring the project back to programme, to accelerate it, to re-plan the availability of resources in view of delays in any one project, or to eliminate the project because it is not worth while to continue with it. In comparing progress, time and costs, it is important that this should be done for each section of the work, stage by stage, as well as for the contract as a whole; otherwise misleading information may be provided. For example, overall total spending may be in line with budget, but stage-by-stage completion may be behind programme.

7.3.1 Progress reports

Project progress reports fall essentially into two classes:

1   Routine reports, including regular (for example monthly) operating statements and more generally based reviews.
2   Periodic reports, coinciding with stage completion assessments or appraisals made by other functional departments; for example, marketing or finance.

   Project operating statements are discussed in Chapter 8 which deals with budgetary control of R&D projects. These statements are concerned to show details of:

1   Budgeted costs in total and for the period in question.
2   Comparison of actual and budgeted costs.
3   Significant variances, with explanations for their occurrence.

There will also be a need for reviews to consider project progress in more general terms. These reviews will include qualitative assessments of achievement which, *inter alia*, will highlight problems which have occurred, estimate the probability of technical success/failure, and consider the action required in the light of revisions to cost or time estimates. A suggested format for such a review is given in Figure 7.6.

In addition to the routine review of project progress, it will also be necessary to take a broad look at progress and potential at periodic intervals. These reviews will aim to include evaluations by those areas of functional management; for example, marketing and finance, which have a direct interest in the prospects of the research programme, but which are not fully represented in the routine reporting system. As progress is attained on each project, marketing and financial plans will begin to crystalise as more accurate predictions become possible. These predictions will be compared with original project appraisals so that the effects of divergence on original plans may be assessed. If divergences are significant, then a complete re-appraisal may be necessary in order to gauge sales as well as financial and technical viability. It is likely that the reviews will best coincide with project stage completions, as these 'milestones' will usually provide a 'hard' base from which to predict likely outcomes. Abrupt fundamental changes in, for example, the market or in the financial structure or status of the company, may have implications which pre-empt all other considerations, and therefore require immediate and 'once and for all' investigation.

7.3.2   Compile a checklist

The following questions may be used as a basis for a useful checklist, which may help to emphasise the points to be covered by the progress reporting system. The reports should make clear to the R&D corporate management the position on the following:

1   *Satisfactory progress*   Progress is as planned and is satisfactory, or whether the project is in trouble and, if so, whether it is thought to be retrievable or irretrievable?
2   *Technical viability*   The project is still technically feasible but further resources are required?
3   *Up-to-date findings*   The results of findings to date include any unexpected discoveries and whether the project needs to be

R&D PROJECT PROGRESS REPORT

Project No. _____

Date _____

Project title:

Cost review:

Cost for period   £ _____   Authorised project cost   £ _____

Planned cost for period   £ _____   Cost to date   £ _____

Period variance   £ _____   Estimated cost to completion £ _____

                                                    Completion cost variance   ____ %

There has been an *improvement/deterioration* in performance against cost

Progress since:

Estimate (gain) loss when compared with programme _____ months

Figure 7.6 R&D project progress report - part 1

R&D PROJECT PROGRESS REPORT - continued

Problems encountered during period: | Estimated date by which problems will be resolved

Estimated effect on programme is _____ months delay

Proposed programme for next period to:
(underline those items not contained in latest revised programme)

Probability of technical failure:

	Original	Now

Original project time _____ months ending on _____

Variance predicted at end of last period _____ %

Variance predicted now _____ %

Revised completion date _____

Recommendation to *proceed with/cancel* project

Prepared by _____ Date _____   Date of next report _____

Figure 7.6 R&D project progress report - part 2

R&D PROJECT PROGRESS REPORT - continued

Project time and cost chart

1 Chart shows the time/cost relationship throughout the project in accordance with the original proposals with the main stage points marked.

2 Chart shows actual performance to date with previous progress report's prediction of future costs and progress through to project completion.

3 Mark up the actual costs incurred during the period

4 Compare cost variance over previous periods and smooth exponentially to obtain new variance.

5 Repeat for time variance.

6 Apply these revised variance values to previous predictions and produce a revised cost/time graph for the remainder of the project.

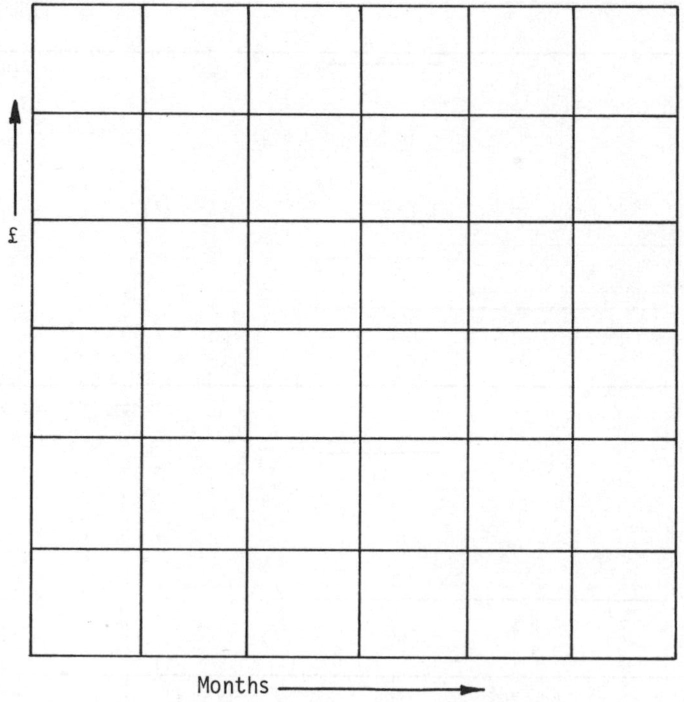

Figure 7.6 R&D project progress report - part 3

| R&D PROJECT PROGRESS REPORT - continued | Project No. _____ |
| | Date _____ |

If either the cost estimate or the time estimate has changed since the previous report, this section must be completed

Cost increase:

Can the Project Cost be kept below the authorised amount? _____

What action can be taken to minimise the cost? _____

What is the minimum total cost estimate? £_____

This action will *extend/reduce* the total project time by ____ months

Time increase:

Can the project be completed on time? _____

If so, at what additional cost? £_____

What action can be taken to minimise delay? _____

What is the estimated completion date on this basis? _____

What is the effect on total cost of *increase/decrease*? £_____

What is the recommended course of action?

What effect will this have on the project justification parameters?

Figure 7.6 R&D project progress report - part 4

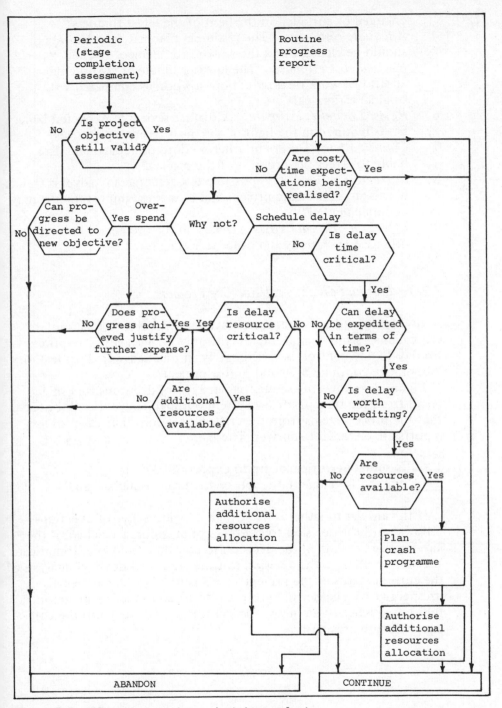

Figure 7.7   R&D project review - decision analysis

enlarged or curtailed in the light of the latest findings?

4   *Adequate resources*   The resources planned are adequate or should be changed and the reasons for changes given?

5   *Revised cost estimate*   The latest estimate of cost includes additional work on a reduction in work, as compared with the original estimates?

6   *Revised benefits estimate*   A further review of expected benefits is required in the light of the most recent discoveries?

7   *Coordination*   Delays in other sections or departments are liable to affect the progress of the project?

8   *Corrective action*   It is possible to overcome any adverse trends in the progress of the project and how these improvements may be implemented?

9   *Effect on other activities*   Delays in the project will affect other R&D sections and other functions?

7.3.3   Elimination of unsatisfactory projects

A vital feature of a project review system is its ability to stimulate critical analysis by management. Not only is this analysis required for day-to-day control, but, ultimately, it must answer the question: 'Should we continue or abandon this project?'

Figure 7.7 shows the sequential analysis of decisions that might result from the type of review system outlined above. It will be seen that the process stems from the critical questions that the progress reports are designed to answer. These are:

1   'Is actual performance up to expectations?' and
2   'Are the fundamental tenets of the project unchanged?'

If the answer to either is 'No', then a logical series of questions follows until the decision to continue or abandon is reached; if the answers are 'Yes', then the decision to continue follows automatically.

Each question in the decision routine requires a detailed analysis of the current status of the project — this is to be expected, because irrespective of whether the project is to be continued or abandoned, the consequence of an incorrect decision can be crucial to the company's future prosperity.

8
BUDGETARY CONTROL OF PROJECTS

8.1 SETTING THE BUDGET

Once the plans have been approved and evaluated they can be put into operation. In this chapter, attention is paid to the basic control 'units', the individual R&D projects. The necessary stages for control are as follows:

1   Breaking down the costs to show how much is to be spent within each budgetary control period.
2   Establishing procedures for collecting costs so that they can be booked to the appropriate projects.
3   Examining the costs incurred and comparing them with the budgeted costs for the work done, and, where appropriate, extracting variances.
4   Preparing reports and statements on R&D projects showing the position to date and any significant variances requiring action.
5   Ensuring that appropriate action is taken to keep spending and results 'on course'.
6   Reviewing each project on a continuous basis, thus detecting any departures from plans as early as possible.

As already emphasised any excess spending will not only affect the financial outcome of a project but also the financial resources available. If in a particular period excess spending continues, there may be difficulty in meeting commitments outside the R&D field.

8.1.1   Breakdown of costs

The costing of individual projects can follow similar lines to those used for conventional job costing. Once a project has been given top priority, and is included in the current year's budget, a technical feasibility study will be required to determine the best methods of approach. This will look at the manpower required together with fixed assets and other facilities, materials, and supplies. The steps covered are shown below:

1   Manpower requirements (labour costs)   The project should be considered in terms of manpower requirements, which would include the appointment of a group leader and other personnel. For simple projects the group leader could be part-time, but with a large scale R&D project it might warrant a full-time leader and research workers from a number of disciplines such as chemistry, biology, engineering and other areas. These requirements should be converted into a manpower estimate, which in turn will be transferred to the budget for the individual project (see Figure 8.1). Where a group leader looks after a number of projects, a decision should be made on how to deal with his salary and related costs. The question of apportioning costs is discussed in other parts of this book.

2   Fixed assets and other facilities required   Where a new project is to be started which requires additional capital expenditure on fixed assets, this should be covered in the capital expenditure budget. On the other hand, where existing facilities are to be used, the question arises as to what proportion of their cost should be charged to the individual project. There are two extreme views on this matter:

a   to treat the facilities as representing fixed assets which cannot be apportioned between projects; or
b   to charge a reasonable amount to each project for the facilities used.

   The arguments for and against these two procedures are similar to those advanced for supporting or rejecting marginal costing. There are many books on this subject, some of which will be found in the bibliography.

ABC Enterprises Limited	Individual project budget	Year: 1972/5

Project description and number: _____

Start: _____ Finish: _____

Cost category	Four-week periods (£)													Year total
	1	2	3	4	5	6	7	8	9	10	11	12	13	
DIRECT LABOUR:														
Draughtsmen														
Engineers														
Technicians														
....														
TOTAL DIRECT LABOUR														
DIRECT MATERIALS:														
Raw materials														
Bought-out components														
Consumables														
....														
TOTAL DIRECT MATERIALS														
TOTAL SUB-CONTRACT CHARGES														
TOTAL REVENUE COSTS														
CAPITAL COSTS														
TOTAL PROJECT COSTS														

Compiled by: _____ Date: _____ Approved by: _____ Date: _____ Revision dates: _____

Figure 8.1 Budget for individual project. Notes: (1) overheads, if directly attributable to individual projects, could could be shown as a separate category of revenue costs; (2) employee numbers might be included in the schedule if circumstances so warrant

124 Whichever method is used, it is important that management is aware of the costs incurred. Laboratory facilities and equipment might be capable of alternative uses, and, if costs are not apportioned to each project, there should at least be some indication that each project using those facilities has a responsibility for the fixed costs. In this way recognition is given to the total costs of operating the R&D function, whereas if the fixed costs are excluded, there is a danger that managers will lose sight of their overall financial responsibilities. There is also the fact that fixed costs are those defined as such by management. Some costs may be capable of being treated as fixed, even though they contain a substantially variable element. A costing system should not allow for apparent avoidance of responsibility by adopting a definition which suits that purpose.

3 *Material requirements* The material requirements would include raw materials, manufactured and bought-out parts, and various other supplies, together with electricity, gas, compressed air and similar services.

These costs together with other miscellaneous expenses which relate to a project, would be included on a suitably designed project form (see Figure 8.1). This illustration shows the type of information required, but for each R&D organisation the format could be designed to meet specific requirements.

8.1.2 Timing of project control

A total budget cost which is not phased over the time period during which the work is to be done and the expenditure is to be incurred will be useless for purposes of control. Control periods should be determined so that comparisons can be made with actual progress at the end of each period; this is explained later in this chapter.

With a complex project, network analysis can be employed to show the time sequence and the order in which each phase of the project must be taken. With R&D there may be difficulty in keeping to the original schedule of operations and therefore a certain amount of flexibility is essential. However, for successful budgetary control an attempt must be made to time the various stages of the projects and link them with their financial implications.

8.1.3 Establishing procedures

The procedures to be used for collecting information for the establish-

ment of project budgets will vary according to the company, its size
and the complexity of its operations. With a simple organisation they
may consist of listing the items involved with the project, and obtaining approval of the total amount. The latter may be done by the
Board, the director of R&D or the managing director. Involvement of
the chief accountant will also be essential, thus checking financial
viability.

Many companies would benefit from some form of committee
structure to consider projects, and to look at the overall costs of both
R&D, and of the major items that make up the R&D programme.
The advantage of this approach is that it enables all interested parties
to become involved in both planning and implementation. Because
R&D is an all-embracing function, there should be representatives
from the various functions – production, marketing, and finance –
to express their points of view.

Prior to detailed consideration of budgets by the budget committee,
the opinions of the R&D project team leaders and other key personnel
should be sought, thus allowing them to participate in the establishment
of the individual budgets. Provided the constraints on spending are
understood, considerable benefit should result from this form of participative management.

In arriving at the individual costs for materials, manpower, and other
likely commitments, the accountant, purchasing department and others
must assist R&D personnel in providing prices, hourly rates, and
other facts necessary to build up the budgets.

8.1.4   Classification and coding

In designing a system for classifying R&D expenditure it is necessary to
use code numbers and standard descriptions, both for individual projects and for the types of expense that make up the costs for each
project. A typical classification is shown in Chapter 12. The necessary
procedures would appear in the accounting manual or other form of
instruction used for explaining the system applied in the company. In
this connection it will be necessary to decide which are the current
costs and which are to be deferred, bearing in mind that wherever
possible costs should be changed in the period in which they are incurred.

As an understanding of cost behaviour is a pre-requisite of effective
budgetary control, it is essential that managers should appreciate the
difference between fixed, semi-variable, and variable costs. In addition,
attention should be paid to what are the normal authorised costs and
what are supplementary, i.e. over and above those originally budgeted.

An understanding of such costs will also assist when, in the last resort, a decision has to be made whether to carry on with the project or to abandon it. Once certain costs are committed, they may be incurred even after the project is abandoned. This could apply where contracts are in existence, or where plant, machinery and other facilities have been made available for a project and are still in existence. Unless an alternative use can be found, the cost of these must be recognised when making the abandonment decision.

8.2 MEASUREMENT AND ANALYSIS OF EXPENDITURE

Control is exercised to secure the achievement of plans. R&D project control has two distinct facets — measurement of actual and planned performance in physical or qualitative terms, and comparison of actual and planned resource consumption in financial terms.

Performance assessment will, in the first instance, derive from control techniques such as bar and Gantt charts and network analyses, as discussed in Chapter 7. Techniques that are designed to control in terms of resource requirements as well as time, for example, PERT, will provide information on such matters as the consumption of technical man-hours up to given stage completions. This information will be set alongside comparisons of actual and budgeted expenditure and the variances from both sources analysed and compared.

Clearly, the common feature of these two facets of project control is the assessment, in whatever terms, of the difference between planned and achieved levels of activity. If costs are likely to fluctuate directly with activity levels, then there may be a case for using flexible budgeting to give accurate measures of efficiency. Circumstances and the ability to distinguish between the fixed and variable costs will dictate the merits or otherwise of using such a system. However, it is important to stress that whether using fixed or flexible budgeting, careful analysis of cost behaviour is vital in determining the extent to which variance analysis may be valid and suitable.

8.2.1   Operating statements for R&D projects

In Chapter 6, reference was made to the need for overall control of functional activities including R&D, the emphasis being on the responsibility of managers to operate their functions within the framework of a corporate budgeting system. In this chapter the analysis is taken a stage further, responsibilities being located around individual projects. A typical project operating statement is given in Figure 8.2. This statement is intended to show all the vital facts relating to the project in question, such as:

ABC Enterprises Limited	R&D PROJECT OPERATING STATEMENT	Period No. _____ Ended _____

Project description and number: _____

This period			Expenditure	Year to date		
Budget £	Actual £	Variance £		Budget £	Actual £	Variance £
			DIRECT LABOUR: Draughtsmen Engineers Technicians			
			DIRECT MATERIALS: Raw materials Bought-out components Consumables			
			DIRECT OVERHEAD (if appropriate)			
			SUB-CONTRACT			
			TOTAL REVENUE EXPENDITURE			
			CAPITAL COSTS: Plant and machinery			
			TOTAL CAPITAL EXPENDITURE			
			TOTAL PROJECT COSTS			

Legend: Variances favourable/(unfavourable). Comments on the variances are not included here but the reasons for the variances should be included in the report

Figure 8.2 Project operating statement

1   Project description.
2   Job number.
3   Budgeted costs in total.
4   Budgeted costs for the period in question.
5   Comparison of actual and budgeted costs.
6   Significant variances.
7   General comments on the overall state of the project and some guidance on whether results and costs are being kept within reasonable levels. A project with no variances may still be unsatisfactory if no tangible results are achieved. The likely benefits from a project must be evaluated in one way or another. This may prove difficult, but unless an attempt is made the variance analysis will be misleading.

The example has been kept very simple. Additional details could include the total costs authorised and the cumulative position.

8.3   CORRECTIVE ACTION

When examining R&D projects, it is necessary to analyse each type of expense and then decide whether additional expenses are necessary, in what area, and whether they can be justified. If so, a supplementary authorisation form will be completed and approved by the appropriate manager. The supplementary figures would then be added to the budget, thus allowing further expenditure to be incurred. If at all possible, retrospective authorisation should be avoided.

If, after work is carried out on a project, there is no sign of any benefit being received within the foreseeable future then it could be decided to abandon the project. This is not an easy decision to make, because this may be an admission of failure. However, it is preferable to abandon a project showing no signs of success and concentrate on the viable projects.

As emphasised in the previous chapter, project operating statements should be read in conjunction with operational reviews. This process will identify any divergence between actual and budgeted progress, with the object of promoting action to currect the situation, and to minimise any likely recurrence.

8.3.1   Post-completion audit of R&D projects

When a project has resulted in the successful development of a new product or method, there is no way initially of knowing whether this will be a market success. Products or methods that appear to show

	Factor weighting	Factor assessment					Final rating
		Very good	Good	Aver-age	Poor	Very poor	

MARKET POSITION
 	
1 Adaptable to existing distri-
  bution channels
2 Fits in with existing products
3 Fits into existing markets
4 Relative position on price and
  quality
5 Sizes and grades available
6 Availability of marketing and
  servicing facilities
7 Market problems
8 Relations with products in range							

PRODUCT LIFE 1 Suitability of demand 2 Size of market 3 Possible cyclical fluctuations 4 Possible seasonal fluctuations 5 Copyright or patentable rights 6 Security of market							

PRODUCTION FACILITIES
 	
1 Can use existing company
  technology and 'know-how'
2 Use of existing machinery
3 Availability of skilled labour
4 Availability of adequate raw
  materials
5 Free from legal restrictions
6 Cost competitiveness							

LONG-TERM PROSPECTS
 	
1 Expected trend of market
  growth
2 Adaptable to technological
  growth
3 Competitive standing							

Figure 8.3 Product assessment checklist

great promise sometimes fade out when put onto the market, but others which were entered into with some scepticism may develop into extremely successful activities.

Because of the unknown factor in the success of a project, it is essential to monitor the overall progress made within a short period of the product launch, and subsequently, annually or more frequently. Only by keeping the matter under review in terms of volume of sales, customer satisfaction, profit margins and other relevant data will it be possible to know whether the R&D function is operating in a manner that allows corporate objectives to be achieved.

A check list for assessing the 'quality' of projects may take the form indicated in Figure 8.3. This may be varied to suit the needs of the specific business. It should indicate the necessary approach for selec ing the best product mix for the market and conditions which exist. Points may be awarded on a suitable scale such as 5 for 'satisfactory', 8 for 'good' and 9 and 10 for 'excellent'.

8.4   LINK WITH COST ACCOUNTING

The outline of a possible project control system is given in this chapter. In practice, it may be necessary to provide a detailed breakdown of the costs incurred, thereby enabling a close watch to be maintained on spending. This would tend to be the case where there is a critical cash shortage or when working within strict limits for an external customer or for a department or company within the business concerned. Chapter 12 deals with the cost accounting procedures for recording R&D expenditure.

9 EVALUATING THE EFFECTIVENESS OF R&D

The benefits to be derived from R&D work are now, perhaps more than ever before, the subject of increasingly rigorous examination. Research and development expenditure has reached such proportions, in both the private and public sectors, that the utility of future research must be seen to satisfy declared objectives and *thereby* justify the necessary allocation of resources. One of the most forceful means by which an R&D department can justify work in a particular sphere, other than by identifying it as essential to survival, is to demonstrate the effectiveness of its previous or existing research in similar or allied fields. This is the situation applicable to most companies constantly seeking to extend, improve, or diversify their product ranges.

In Chapter 2, the three principal areas of R&D activity were outlined as basic research, applied research and development work. It is necessary, therefore, to establish a framework of criteria against which the effectiveness of these three areas of activity can be evaluated both independently and in aggregate.

9.1 APPRAISAL OF COMPLETED PROJECTS

When is a research or development project complete? Some will argue that certain research, particularly of the basic type, is never completed or is at least of such a long-term nature that the concept is valueless. Similarly, others propound that the diverse 'spin-off' benefits of research can be neither adequately quantified nor capable of collation, and therefore, appraisal of total effectiveness is incomplete. Such arguments do not negate the desirability of evaluation, but merely serve to emphasise some reservations or assumptions required to accompany it.

A research or development project can usually be regarded as *complete* when, for example, one or more of the following conditions apply:

1   When an existing product which has been developed to incorporat certain new technical features is of a form suitable for manufactur
2   When an entirely new product becomes ready for sale.
3   When an idea has been pursued to the point where manufacture is a theoretical possibility (although here the development stage may not be fully complete).
4   When the finance available for it has been fully consumed. This may mean abandoning a project so 'completion' is really termination.
5   When independent research in the same field has already been pursued to its logical conclusion and no future refinements are possible.

It is clear from the above examples that the setting of the time hori-zons for research projects may appear to be an essentially arbitrary process, but may be logical under particular circumstances. Thus in the case of example (5), which will often apply to basic research projects, the completion date is logical with respect to the availability of resources.

The utility evaluation of a completed project is the final phase of an ongoing process or system of appraisal. In Chapter 5 the initial phase was considered − the project feasibility study, and the applicatic of investment appraisal techniques. In Chapters 6 and 8, the technique of budgetary control and exception reporting were explained in the context of the monitoring and control phase of the appraisal system. Finally comes the completion evaluation − the phase presently being considered.

9.1.1   The elements of evaluation of completed R&D projects

There are three elements in the evaluation of an individual or series of completed R&D projects; namely;

1   *Comparison of objectives*   Reference to, and comparison with the
    original objectives.
2   *Impact of achievements*   Examination of the current and future
    impact of the work achieved.
3   *Systems review*   Review of the systems and organisation in the
    R&D function.

The first two elements are concerned with examining the effectiveness
of the output achieved by the commitment of resources to the
function; the third with the planning, organisation and control framework within which the research and development team has operated.

9.1.2   Relating results to objectives

The relationship of R&D activity to corporate objectives was discussed
in Chapter 4. Basic and applied research, together with development
work, constitutes a critical determinant of a company's ability to set
and attain meaningful objectives. The importance of designing comprehensive strategy to meet objectives was explained, also the role of
techniques such as technological forecasting in the development of
detailed plans. Similarly, in Chapter 5, it was noted that initial project
selection techniques incorporate certain criteria designed to test
whether a proposed line of research has the strategic 'qualifications'
to satisfy the desired corporate objectives.
    For a realistic assessment of progress made, the objectives of each
project, originally specified at the planning and approval stage, should
now be compared with achievements. The first test of effectiveness
is therefore, 'Has the project *in fact* measured up to the original expectations included in the initial evaluation?' The answer to this
question will be largely apparent whilst monitoring the latter stages
of the project development. Nevertheless, it requires formal overview
at the completion date.
    Some companies have developed a system of Management by
Objectives (MbO) to deal with R&D in a way that allows jobs to be
analysed and then planned and controlled.
    The precise manner in which this may be adopted depends upon
the size of company and its problems. Essentially it means breaking
down the entire R&D function into recognisable 'responsibility
centres' and, at the lower levels showing the necessary detail for
effective control of the objectives. In stages the processes involved
may be as follows:

1   *Showing broad responsibilities*   Draw an organisation chart to
    show the main responsibilities. This aspect is considered in

Chapter 3. It is essential that any chart should be realistic and kept up-to-date.

2   *MbO descriptive manual*   In a large company there will be need for written instructions on how the system is to operate. The intention is to advocate and motivate: given the reasons for the approach and its aims there is a good chance that research personnel will respond. Without guidance they are likely to pursue objectives which are not part of an integrated plan.

3   *Devise improvement plans*   This may be looked upon as a means of getting the best out of company resources. It involves a number of stages, principally:

  a   analysis of each job;
  b   agree objectives for *(i)* departments and *(ii)* individuals;
  c   write job descriptions for each person.

These become the basis of the plans and can be used for monitoring future progress.

4   *Control the work*   This should be done in terms of quality and quantity. Often there is difficulty, but with a blend of objectives and, where appropriate, subjective judgement, it should be possible to measure the progress which is being made. Suitable forms and statements can be designed to compare objectives with actual achievements.

9.1.3   Forms and procedures

The forms and procedures to be used may be along the lines indicated in other parts of this book, particularly in Chapters 7, 8, 9, 12 and 13. They can be adopted to meet the specific requirements. Those which are of direct relevance to this chapter are now explained.

Job Analysis   For successful development of objectives combined with improvement plans, there should be a constructive approach made to detailed job analysis. Unfortunately, this is not a process which is easily accomplished without a full understanding of the work to be done and its related problems. Initially there are bound to be disappointments, including many research workers who do not understand or agree with the job descriptions which allegedly describe their work.

The job analysis may be broken down into a number of stages; often the following are used:

1   Job description.
2   Control areas.
3   Improvement plan.

The *job description* may show the name of the person, age, qualifi-

```
JOB DESCRIPTION FORM                                        Date:_____

Function:  R&D              Department:   Instrument Control
Name:      Dr M. Jones      Joining date: 12 January 19..
Position:  Head of Department   Grade:    VI
```

Job description:

1 FUNCTION AND BROAD RESPONSIBILITIES

Head of Department responsible to Director of R&D for day-to-day operations.

2 CONTROL OVER R&D PROJECTS

2.1 Originate research projects in Instrument Control.
2.2 Improve existing products and systems.
2.3 To study problems of flow, its measurement and control.
2.4 To co-operate with the production manager on problems of flow
    instrumentation.

3 DEALING WITH NEW YORK

3.1 To initiate new work and obtain necessary approvals.
3.2 To plan the work and establish priorities.
3.3 To ensure that new work is assigned to appropriate personnel and
    progress monitored.

4 STAFF SUPERVISION

4.1 To check the work and give necessary assistance.
4.2 To make recommendations on the effective utilisation of staff

5 RESOURCES RESPONSIBILITY

5.1 To recommend necessary materials required
5.2 To justify expenditure on equipment and fixed assets.

6 RECRUITMENT AND DEVELOPMENT OF STAFF

6.1 To recommend on types and numbers of staff.
6.2 To maintain management development plans for each person.
6.3 To recommend attendance at conferences.

7 OTHER RESPONSIBILITIES/DUTIES

7.1 To maintain adequate liaison with outside bodies who are conducting
    research into instrumentation and control systems.

Figure 9.1 Job description form

cations, position held and a detailed breakdown of the duties and
responsibilities. A simplified example is given in Figure 9.1.

The control areas section of the job analysis would include the key
tasks or objectives; the suggested method of achievement and the
time schedule for completion. This is an important foundation for
subsequent control, but it should also be augmented by the use of
financial or cost performance indicators. If a key task has been completed two months early this may be splendid news. However, if the
costs incurred are far in excess of those budgeted, a quite different
interpretation might ensue. Achievements without reference to
sacrifices are of limited value.

In drawing up an *improvement plan* attention should be focussed
on those aspects of the work which can be defined as the improvement of existing products, services, methods or other aspects. They
should be capable of being achieved within a reasonable period of
time such as a year. The method of achievement and likely time scale
and costs should also be given.

9.1.4   Example of control function

> *Develop a method for photographing oil paintings for high
> quality reproduction in the form of prints, but avoiding glare
> and the consequent 'specs' on the reproduction. Completion
> date: April 19. . .*

CONTROL: In May 19. . consider whether objective has been
achieved or, if not, whether to allow a further specified period or
whether to discontinue. Examine improvements which have been
made and assess the extent of the work in relation to the objective
giving some kind of quantitative evaluation, e.g. 100 per cent successful or break the work down into essential expectations:

1   'Specs' not present on majority of pictures with light-coloured
    background: 8 points.
2   Ditto, with medium-coloured background: 9 points.
3   Ditto, with dark-coloured background: 20 points.

Other tests may also be applied, such as trueness of colour achieved
on prints, again giving points for expectations and subsequently to
the actual results achieved, thus allowing *progress comparisons* to be
made. Any wide deviations from the standards set may call for
abandonment of the project. At this stage, before making a final
decision, it will also be desirable to look at the possibility of effecting
improvements.

Each of these major activities could be broken down further into

sub-activities. How far this should be done depends on the nature and
size of the project. If complex and large, it may be feasible for each
activity to be divided into, say, five sub-activities.

9.2   THE PROJECT COST PICTURE APPROACH

The project cost picture approach (a term suggested by Snyder [10])
may be adopted.This method is divided into three stages:
1   *Establishing objectives at the planning stage and then assessing*
    progress on the appropriate due dates.
2   *Assessing progress of each project in terms of the current year's*
    expenditure.
3   *Assessing progress of each project to date by examining:*
    a   *total actual cost in relation to budgeted cost;*
    b   *any necessary revisions and modifications and their effect*
          upon progress and costs.
An important question to resolve is the size and extent of the control
area to be covered by the analysis. Simply comparing predetermined
and actual figures in *global* terms is unlikely to give effective control.
Instead, an attempt should be made to divide a project into 'control
activities', thus allowing monitoring to take place on a time and
quantitative basis.

   In its most basic form, the *control activities* for applied R&D may
be as follows:

1   *Conception and preliminary planning stage*   Define objectives,
    assess the work load, stipulate the period allowed for each
    activity, any other necessary preliminary work.
2   *Effecting plans made*   Carry out the plans and systematically
    work towards the objectives; if possible produce the results
    required within defined time limits.
3   *Test and appraise the results*   Test and modify the results of
    the project to date and assess the degree of success achieved.
4   *Commercial exploitation*   Move into full production and prepare
    to market the product.

The various facts shows are:

1   Figure 9.2, comparison of budgeted cost and revised budget
    (job estimate).
2   Figure 9.3, comparison of budgeted expenditure, actual expen-
    diture and projected actual expenditure (latest estimate).
3   Figure 9.4, comparison of actual expenditure and latest esti-
    mated expenditure with revised budgeted expenditure (job
    estimate).

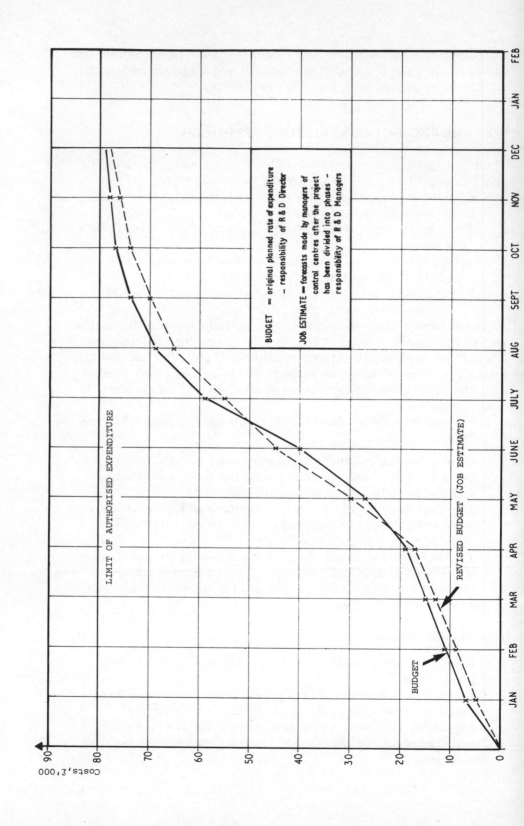

LIMIT OF AUTHORISED EXPENDITURE

BUDGET = original planned rate of expenditure
– responsibility of R & D Director

JOB ESTIMATE = forecasts made by managers of
control centres after the project
has been divided into phases –
responsibility of R & D Managers

REVISED BUDGET (JOB ESTIMATE)

BUDGET

Costs, £'000

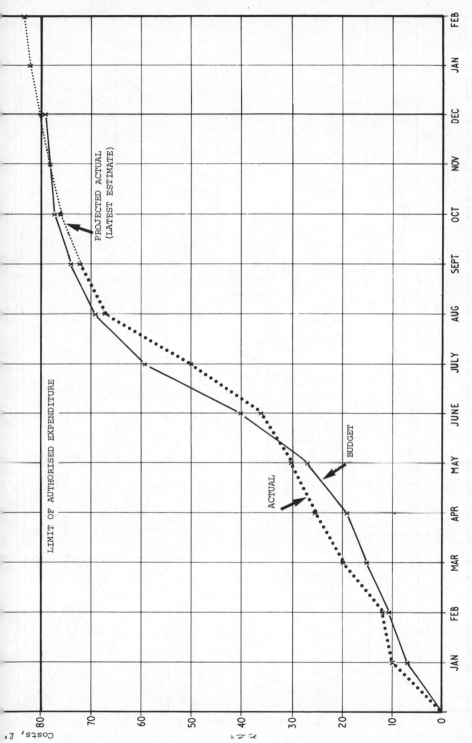

Figure 9.3 Comparison of budgeted expenditure, actual expenditure and projected actual expenditure (latest estimate)

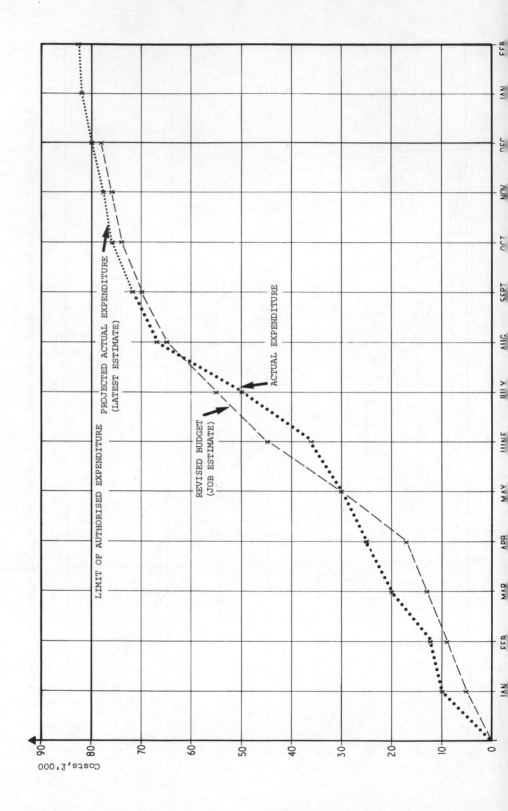

LIMIT OF AUTHORISED EXPENDITURE

PROJECTED ACTUAL EXPENDITURE
(LATEST ESTIMATE)

REVISED BUDGET
(JOB ESTIMATE)

ACTUAL EXPENDITURE

Costs, £'000

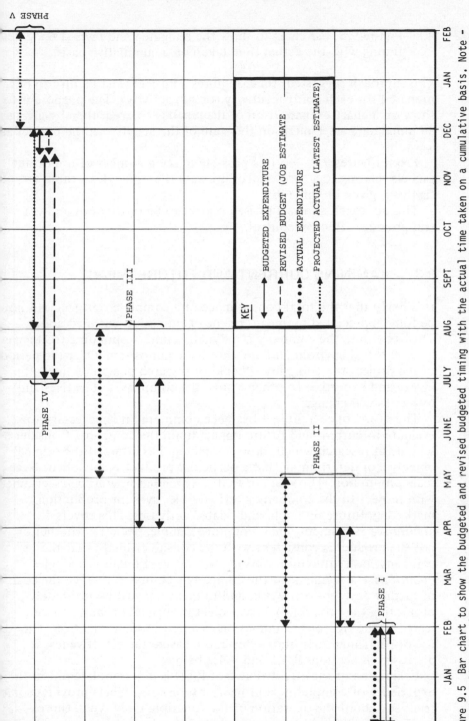

Figure 9.5 Bar chart to show the budgeted and revised budgeted timing with the actual time taken on a cumulative basis. Note – this chart links the first three charts; for example, Phase II was budgeted to take two months for completion at a cumulative cost of £19,000 whilst in actual fact it took three months to complete at a cumulative cost of £30,000

KEY

→ BUDGETED EXPENDITURE

→ REVISED BUDGET (JOB ESTIMATE)

→ ACTUAL EXPENDITURE

→ PROJECTED ACTUAL (LATEST ESTIMATE)

PHASE I
PHASE II
PHASE III
PHASE IV
PHASE V

Costs, £

0 10 20 30 40 50 60 70 80

JAN FEB MAR APR MAY JUNE JULY AUG SEPT OCT NOV DEC JAN FEB

4   Figure 9.5, bar chart to show the budgeted and revised budgeted timing with the actual time taken on a cumulative basis.

The approach suggested, then, requires a Project Cost Picture to be prepared for each control activity (or sub-activity). The purpose is to show on a chart a comparison of the results achieved, thereby giving an immediate assessment on the state of the activity on the project as a whole.

From Figures 9.2—9.5 it is possible to see a number of important aspects relating to a project. To illustrate the principles a table of figures is given in Table 9.1.

This approach allows a revised budget to be introduced and yet still provides effective control.

9.3   EXAMINING CURRENT AND FUTURE IMPACT

It is likely that the total consequence of a completed project will not be fully appreciated by means of the examination outlined above. This is because the company is a dynamic unit, responding to changes in its external environment and internal composition. Over the period of the project the company's 'bank' of research personnel may alter in size and expertise. In other words, the company's objectives and resources will change.

Therefore, once a project has been completed it is necessary to evaluate its current and future impact upon the company. Consider a scheme of research which, now completed, has attained the original objective of determining that a particular product is capable of large scale production. The value of that research has now to be ascertained with respect to the company's revised objectives for production, marketing, future research, and related activities. This covers *qualitative* assessment, including, for example, deciding whether or not the product is consistent with the consumer image that the company has acquired or is trying to achieve. Equally it includes *quantitative* assessment of the company's ability to finance the cost of further development work, and to make a profit by ultimately promoting the product. A new project is born and it must be subjected to the rigorous examination of a new initial evaluation. The use of particular quantitative tests to measure the effectiveness is discussed in Sections 9.4.1 and 9.4.2 below.

Evaluation of the effectiveness of R&D is not complete unless the experience of completing a project or series of projects provides some feedback about the operation of the function. Only when this experience is obtained can any conclusions be drawn about the efficiency of the R&D organisation, the sufficiency of its long- and short-term

TABLE 9.1 R&D costs: authorised limit of expenditure £80,000

	Jan	Feb	Mar	Apr	May	Jun	Jul	Aug	Sep	Oct	Nov	Dec	Jan	Feb
BUDGETED RATE OF EXPENDITURE, £'000														
Expenditure this month	7	4	4	4	8	13	19	10	5	3	1	1		
Cumulative	7	11	15	19	27	40	59	69	74	77	78	79		
REVISED BUDGET (JOB ESTIMATE)														
Expenditure this month	5	4	4	4	13	15	10	10	5	4	2	2		
Cumulative	5	9	13	17	30	45	55	65	70	74	76	78		
ACTUAL EXPENDITURE (Jan-Sep); LATEST ESTIMATE (Oct-Feb														
Expenditure this month	10	2	8	5	5	6	14	17	5	4	2	2	2	1
Cumulative	10	12	20	25	30	36	50	67	72	76	78	80	82	83

DATES OF COMPLETION

Phase	I	II	III	IV	V
Budget	28/2	30/4	31/7	30/11	31/12
Revised budget	28/2	30/4	31/7	30/11	31/12
Actual	28/2	31/5	31/8	31/12	28/2

COSTS BY PHASES

(a) Individual phases

	I	II	III	IV	V
Budget	11	8	40	19	1
Revised budget	9	8	38	21	2
Actual	12	18	37	12	4

(b) Cumulative

	I	II	III	IV	V
Budget	11	19	59	78	79
Revised budget	9	17	55	76	78
Actual	12	30	67	79	83

planning, and the quality of its forecasting and project evaluation techniques. It is these factors which are crucial in determining the ultimate success of the activity.

Regular monitoring of research projects will provide many clues as to whether the organisation is properly geared to achieving the target results. Nevertheless, it is essential to take 'snapshots' of the whole of the R&D activity at periodic intervals, to ensure that the organisation is responding to objectives such as maintaining the desired equilibrium between different areas of research or development. By the nature of such work it is logical to take these 'snapshots' upon completion of each project, but this will depend upon the individual company's circumstances and the nature of the work.

In Section 9.1.2 it was stated that the first test of effectiveness of a research project is whether or not it matches up to the expectations incorporated in the initial project evaluation. In Chapter 5 it was explained how certain appraisal techniques can be applied to these expectations in order to assist in the 'go' or 'no-go' decision for a particular project. Once the actual outcome is known and related to the initial evaluation, it becomes possible to form some judgement and the merits or de-merits of the appraisal technique. For example, the original expectations of variability of outcome or resource commitment may be unrealistically low, and experience may therefore indicate that the parameters for future appraisals should incorporate wider margins of safety.

9.4   RETURN ON R&D EXPENDITURE

The need for evaluating the effectiveness of R&D activity and the framework within which that evaluation should be conducted have been considered. But what are the specific measures available to management to gauge the productivity of R&D? They fall into two classes; namely:

1   Those which compare research income and expenditure to arrive at a performance indicator or statement of return.
2   Those which compare research expenditure with various forms of 'output' to provide indices of causal effect.

The measures may be extracted from the records kept by accountants. Financial operating statements can be designed to reveal significant figures and related ratios. However, there are likely to be problems in producing adequate information and in its interpretation. With the future expectations so uncertain, it is likely that any figures produced will have to be regarded with caution. Nonetheless, they provide the

only objective measures of progress and, used sensibly, can enable
R&D to be channelled in the most appropriate directions.

9.4.1   The problems of measurement

The objectives of quantitative evaluation are to measure the effectiveness of R&D activity with respect to:

1   The status of the company in its external environment, e.g.
     leadership of an industry or simply a significant share of the
     market.
2   The benefits derived from the allocation of resources to other
     corporate activities, e.g. production and marketing.

Essentially, the measures must be able to answer the question —
'Have the additional resources put into research paid a higher return
than could have been obtained by investing elsewhere?' Two fundamental problems apply to all available indicators that purport to
measure effectiveness; namely:

1   As all corporate functions are so inextricably intertwined, how
     is the contribution from R&D to be measured separately from
     all others?
2   In view of the highly variable and often unpredictable time lag
     or gestation period between the start of research into a particular
     idea and that idea's ultimate contribution to profits, how can
     meaningful comparison of costs and benefits be adequately
     made?

Certain of the ratios and financial statements commonly used attempt
to overcome the first problem by adopting a marginal or incremental
approach; that is, identifying the additional contribution to profits
afforded by R&D which would not have been realised had research
not been undertaken. The correctness of this approach rests on the
presumption that other activities such as marketing or production
continue to contribute uniformly to the profit of new and old products alike, and that is equal efforts are given to each of the two
classes of products, they would produce similar results. It is
unnecessary to examine this presumption in detail except to say that
advertising, selling policies, and production techniques are just a few
of the factors which have constantly changing effects upon profitability.
    There is the problem of a time lag between effort and results, but
the effects may be overcome, or at least minimised by:

1   Bearing in mind the industry average, estimate the average
     gestation period for the company (referred to above), and use
     this to relate costs and benefits. And/or
2   Employing a cumulative moving average of significant figures
     such as the ratio of total research costs to total profits.

In employing these techniques, an attempt is being made to correlate
costs and benefits as accurately as possible, whilst simultaneously
smoothing the relevant indicator to even out the 'lumpiness' of
random variations.

9.4.2   The measures of effectiveness

The class of measures for comparison of research income and expenditure include the following:

1   A surplus or deficit shown on an operating statement arising
     from a comparison of research costs incurred, and recoveries
     obtained through charging R&D work to user departments in
     the company, or to outside bodies.
2   The return on capital employed obtained by expressing the
     surplus or deficiency in (1) above as a percentage of the assets
     employed by the R&D department.
3   An index of profitability, as shown in Table 9.2.

The index is obtained by expressing R&D revenues, calculated in-
crementally as shown in Section 9.4.1, as a multiple of R&D costs.
There is an important difference between the research profit and loss
statement shown and a conventional statement prepared for financial
reporting purposes. The statement includes an estimate of total
future revenues from each product as well as realised revenues.
Future revenues are discounted back to present values before being
added to realised revenues. Total earnings are assigned to the years
in which the research effort was undertaken and the earned revenue
figures are updated and made more accurate as each year passes.
    The second class of measure provided comparison of research
expenditure with various forms of 'output'. These are:

1   The ratio of research costs to total company profits.
2   The percentage of total company profits contributed by new
     products.
3   The percentage share of the market related to research costs.
4   Research costs related to sales growth.
5   Research costs per employee.

TABLE 9.2 Statement of research contribution to corporate profits   *147*

Year	Total research income £	Total research expense £	Net research contribution £	Index of return
1970	6100	4200	1900	1.5
1971	7200	4600	2600	1.6
1972	5400	5100	300	1.1
1973	7000	5700	1300	1.2
1974	3800	6000	(2200)	0.6
1975	6000	6100	(100)	1.0
1976	8200	6200	2000	1.3
TOTAL 70-76	43700	37900	5800	1.2

Other performance indicators may be used, but it is essential that whatever measure is employed it must be based upon the existence of a clear casual relationship between the input and output of the R&D activity. Where the relationship is complicated by the effects of time or non-R&D functions, then the limitations inherent in the indicator must be explicitly stated when a judgement of effectiveness is formed.

10
ACCOUNTING TREATMENT OF R&D EXPENDITURE

The treatment of research and development expenditure in published accounts raises two sources of potential difficulty. On the one hand, there is no general definition of the term, and on the other, there is no statutory obligation to disclose the information, however defined. (This is now covered in *Statement of Standard Accounting Practice, No. 2 Disclosure of Accounting Policies*), published by the Institute of Chartered Accountants of England and Wales. It is *recommended* that the basis for charging R&D should be re-examined. ED14 proposes that the annual expenditure incurred be stated in the published accounts.)

The scope of R&D and its conceptual delineation into basic research, applied research and development was explained in Chapter 2. The identification of basic and applied research expenditure should not present difficulty, but the expression 'development expenditure' is often used in a wider sense than the conceptual definition implies.

There is evidence of disparity in the policies adopted by companies for the disclosure of R&D activity. Some companies disclose information, although its nature and extent vary from case to case, whilst other companies make no explicit disclosure. Some companies write off the total expenditure against the trading profits of the year in which it is incurred. In other cases the expenditure is carried forward as an asset until such time as development is complete, and it is then written off by instalments based on the probably life of the product created.

Theoretically there should be a matching of expected benefits with expenditure incurred. This could mean costs incurred in the current year may quite legitimately be spread over the next, say, three years. In practice, wherever possible, a more prudent policy would be to charge the expenditure in the accounts each year, thereby avoiding the creation of fictitious assets.

10.1 DEFINITION OF DISCLOSED R&D EXPENDITURE

In practice the definition of R&D expenditure adopted by a particular company, depends upon its own internal organisation. The organisation of the R&D department will be based on the decision as to whether the activity is to be operated on functional or other lines, such as by project. All expenses of an R&D department, and some other departments might be classified as R&D expenditure. For example, the Chairman's Review for 1972 of Pilkington Brothers Limited, describes the company's R&D activity in some detail and, in particular, states 'The straight total of R&D revenue expenditure, identified as R&D, is about £6 million, . . .; there is undoubtedly much more included in works cost and not separately identified'.

Apart from the influence of organisational structure on the definition of R&D, the *nature* of the relevant expenses will determine whether they are to be classified as R&D. The *Surveys of Published Accounts* published by the Institute of Chartered Accountants, discusses many types of expense which are often described as 'development'. These include:

1 Starting-up expenses of new factories or plant before production commences.
2 Market development.
3 Plantation development.
4 Expenditure of prototypes.
5 Systems development in connection with computer installations.

The surveys emphasise that the nature of the expense is often not made clear in the accounts of the companies concerned, although disclosure is now improving.

In an unpublished research paper entitled *Study of Accounting for R&D Expenditure* (prepared for a research committee of the Institute of Chartered Accountants in England and Wales), a survey was made of the practices and attitudes towards R&D of approximately twenty large companies. On the problem of definition, the following conclusion was reached: 'Some companies treat all produce development up to and including the building of a prototype as R&D, others the development up to but not including building of a prototype. Some companies regard work on improvements to existing products as R&D, others do not.'

10.1.1 Some examples of the definition of R&D Expenditure (taken from published accounts)

Example 1   British Leyland Motor Corporation Limited   R&D is defined as: 'all research and development expenditure, including, the design and production of prototypes of new models'.

Example 2   Fisons Limited   R&D includes: 'expenditure incurred in the operation of major new plant during the period between its installation and the achievement of normal operational efficiency and in connection with the establishment of markets for new products'.

Example 3   Pilkington Brothers Limited   'The R&D revenue expenditure covers four categories of activity:
  (i)   maintaining the research laboratories including the basic administrative and technical services;
  (ii)   technical support to the current activities of a division;
  (iii) R&D in existing products and processes;
  (iv)   R&D in new products and processes.'

10.2   POLICIES OF ACCOUNTING TREATMENT FOR R&D EXPENDITURE

A company engaged in R&D has open to it, two alternative methods of accounting treatment: deferral or write-off.

10.2.1   Deferral — matching future expenditure and benefits

R&D expenditure is charged to a control account (or accounts) and then a decision is made on the amount to be written off in a specific accounting year. This is an attempt to match expenditure incurred with benefits — preferably revenues — arising from the work done. If a company spends £1 million on developing a new product which is expected to sell at a profitable level over the next three years as a

minimum, a decision may be made to write off that amount over the
period. After three years it may be reasonable to suppose that further
research or development may be necessary. In any event, even if costs
are to be deferred, because of the uncertainties of the future, there is
unlikely to be any circumstances where deferment could be justified
for a period in excess of three years. The theoretical and practical
considerations are examined in greater detail later in this chapter.

10.2.2   Write-off each year

To write off R&D expenditure in the profit and loss account as and
when it is incurred, irrespective of when the revenues directly attributable to the expenditure are actually realised and credited to the
profit and loss account. This method has the considerable advantage
of clearing the R&D expenditure each year. It represents a clear cut
approach which is easily understood without the complication of
deferring costs into a future year in the form of fictitious assets.

10.2.3   Conventions of accounting

It is beneficial to examine the background relating to the general
procedures followed in dealing with expenditure such as R&D. Once
the general principles are understood, they can be applied to develop
a policy for dealing with the expenditure in question. Accountants
have formulated a number of rules or conventions for dealing with
costs and revenues, and these are as follows:

1   Perpetual existence   The assumption made is that a company
will continue to operate indefinitely. Under normal circumstances
there is no question of anticipating that the business will come to an
end. Rather, a company is assumed to have a perpetual existence and
therefore attention should be paid to what is likely to happen in the
future, where appropriate providing for contingencies which will
affect the results. This could be construed to emphasise that costs
may be deferred because essentially R&D is a long-term activity, but
such a simplified assumption can rarely be substantiated.

2   Matching of costs and revenues   When calculating the results of
individual years, the revenues for one year should be compared with
costs for the same period. If this is not done with reasonable accuracy,
then the residual figure, the profit, will not be a true reflection of
what has occurred. This principle divides into two related aspects:
a   the *accruals concept* which requires that any items due but un-

paid for a period should be included by way of provision;
b   the *costs and benefits matching concept* which calls for consideration of the expected results of spending specific sums on R&D.

Matching costs and benefits is the more difficult problem. With R&D expenditure there may be difficulty in ascertaining how much of the cost is attributable to a particular year. Often an individual project is not capable of assessment in terms of increased revenues or profits, which means that subjective opinions arise as to how much cost should be written off in a year.

3   Consistency   Once a policy or method has been established, this should be used consistently and not changed from one period to another to give different accounting results. This principle is extremely important and yet difficult to apply when related to R&D. Consistency implies that what has happened previously will establish a pattern for the future; there is, therefore, a basis to follow when writing off R&D expenditure.

Unfortunately, R&D expenditure does not always produce the expected benefits, nor is there likely to be standard pattern in terms of the amount to be spent and the profits or extra revenue which result. How then can consistency be obtained when there is uncertainty regarding the results to be achieved? Often the best solution is to fall back on the best commonsense approach for the circumstances which prevail, remembering that it is usually more realistic and prudent to write off costs as soon as possible.

10.3   DEVELOPING A COMPANY POLICY FOR R&D EXPENDITURE

How R&D expenditure is dealt with within specific companies must be determined by the circumstances that prevail, and the judgement of the board of directors and financial advisers. Guidelines which may be used when determining policy are as follows:

1   Where the research expenditure applies to work of a general nature and not to specific projects, it should be written off to the profit and loss account in the year in question.
2   Where research expenditure relates to a specific project and where development expenditure relates to a product or project from which future revenues are expected, the amounts concerned *may* be carried forward into a future accounting period.

This does not mean that the expenditure should necessarily be carried
forward, although following the 'matching principle' discussed earlier,
if benefits are expected in the future, then the cost could be charged
against future years. What should be made clear is that where expenditure is to be carried forward, there should be a *strong* probability
that revenue will accrue from future sales of new projects or services.
If there is any doubt on this matter, it would be better to write off
the expenditure as and when it is incurred. Because of the nature of
R&D activities, even if a large sum is spent in a particular year, there
is no guarantee of success. A company may find that a large amount
has been expended, but the commercial results are negligible. In this
case, there can be no question of applying the 'matching rule' simply
because there is no expected revenue. Other considerations must
apply; for example:

1   Should a single year be burdened with expenditure which,
    strictly speaking, has no bearing on the trading results of that
    period?
2   What is the nature of the 'cost' incurred; would it be better
    treated as a form of special loss and written off immediately
    or over a number of years?
3   Should the profit or loss for a period be distorted by charging
    costs which do not represent economically justifiable
    expenditure?

Some accountants would prefer to see such costs spread over a
number of years, thus 'equalising' the profit earned. In turn, this
should represent a fairer distribution of the special costs and allow
valid comparisons to be made from one period to another. If this
approach is adopted, care should be taken to ensure that the impact
of R&D on the liquidity position is fully understood by the board.
When the profit and cash flow positions are out of step there is a
danger that a liquidity crisis will not be detected in time to take
corrective action.

   If the company adopts the more conservative approach of writing
off expenditure each year, it is likely they are pursuing a sounder
policy. The size of the profit in the year in question will tend to
affect the attitude of shareholders. If the charging of R&D expenditure
changes a profit into a loss there may be resentment. However, the
concern should be with calculating a profit which represent a true
and fair view of the operations in the year in question. A special
note in the accounts could indicate the extraordinary nature of the
R&D expenditure and its effect on profit. This would then allow
shareholders and other interested parties to judge for themselves the
success or otherwise of the company's policy.

When expenditure is deferred for writing off in a future period, the company is burdening future years with expenditure which may not produce tangible results. From a financial management point-of-view too large a figure for R&D carried forward in this way is a sign of weakness, both in terms of financial stability and, possibly, in the management of the company. If there is difficulty in producing tangible results from the R&D projects, there might be a weakness in the planning procedures for controlling and reviewing the work in these areas.

If R&D expenditure which relates to specific products or projects, is done at the request of the customer, there may be justification for carrying forward the costs incurred. Usually in such circumstances, there is a contract against which to charge the customer with the amount concerned and it would be correct therefore to treat the amount as a long-term contract.

10.3.1 Disclosure in the accounts

Where a company has incurred R&D expenditure which is expected to produce future sales revenues, as indicated earlier, the costs incurred could be deferred and carried forward on the balance sheet. Generally, the deferred expenditure should be shown separately in a *special asset account* with a title such as 'Research and Development Expenditure Account'. The balance on the account would be shown on the Balance Sheet and would represent a 'fictitious asset'. The latter description emphasises the nature of R&D expenditure and the reason for a sound policy on its treatment. Carrying forward deferred costs when there is some uncertainty on their future revenue-producing potential is misleading and against sound accounting principles.

The progress made on projects should be considered when decisions are being made on whether costs ought to be deferred. If applied research is continuing and prospects of success are high, there may well be justification for deferral *provided* a satisfactory amount is being charged each year. There are unlikely to be circumstances where a company can justify deferment of all R&D costs for an indefinite period. In the statement of *accounting policies* there should be an explanation of how R&D expenditure is being treated; what the deferred costs represent and what degree of success is being achieved. It is the latter which is of vital importance; if the rate is low it means that the bulk of research costs are really losses and should not be deferred at all.

In describing the nature of the expenditure, the rules for dealing with it should be borne in mind. As a minimum requirement, the main classes of expenditure should be categorised, thus enabling rational decisions to be made on the treatment of each one. There would have to be considerable justification for deferring R&D costs relating to pure or basic research which has been abandoned or is of a continuing nature. In these circumstances, there is generally difficulty in establishing a causal relationship between costs incurred and future benefits and, therefore, an immediate write off is the most desirable course of action. There is also the added factor that such research will usually be part of a planned programme and as such the costs should not fluctuate widely from one year to another. The annual outlay can be written off within the year in which it is incurred without the complication of deferment.

A substantial development project may be treated differently, but there is still no hard and fast rule on whether to defer or not. If in doubt, the correct approach is to dispose of the costs. Where, after careful assessment, it appears that the costs of a project are capable of being deferred, then they can be transferred to an asset account. Considerations which would determine the eligibility are as follows:

1   Amount of the expenditure – it would have to be substantial to justify deferral, usually over and above normal annual expenditure.
2   Evidence of the development of products or services which will earn significant revenues in future periods.
3   Acceptance by the board that the project (or projects) is important in relation to the achievement of the main objectives of the company.

This expenditure can then be deferred for a reasonable period, writing off an appropriate amount each year.

The deferred costs should not be carried forward indefinitely. Correct accounting procedure requires a statement as to how it is intended to treat the balance on the account. Although there is no hard and fast rule on the maximum period to be covered, anything in excess of three to five years should not be taken, because in these circumstances it is difficult to forecast the likely outcome with accuracy. In any event, if it becomes clear that profits are available for the purpose, an attempt should be made to write off expenditure earlier than anticipated.

Sometimes circumstances arise where it is thought that benefits from specific R&D expenditure will accrue evenly over, say, the next five years, but actual results of the earlier years may bring about more revenue than anticipated, with the opportunity for the costs incurred to be written off quicker than expected.

Whether the deferral or write-off method of accounting treatment is chosen, will depend on a number of factors including:

1   The absolute volume and/or significance of the R&D activity as expressed, for example, by the expenditure incurred.
2   The intrinsic nature of the expenditure incurred.
3   The accounting treatment of expenditure having similar time/profit characteristics, e.g. product launch expenses.
4   The policies generally adopted within particular industries.
5   The desire to be prudent when reporting profits.
6   The objectives of accruing profits evenly in order to establish a stable dividend policy.
7   The extent to which R&D activity is a temporary or permanent feature of the company's operations.

This list is not exhaustive, but an examination of the R&D function set against these and other suitable criteria, should enable management to form a view as to the most suitable method of treatment.

In addition, the advantages and disadvantages of each accounting method will influence the decision, and these are summarised below.

10.4.1 Deferral

1 Advantages:
a   the method avoids the distorting effect on profits caused by the time lag between the incidence of R&D expenditure and attributable income;
b   the stabilising effect on profits will minimise share price fluctuations, which might otherwise result from wide profit fluctuation and will enable the development of a sound dividend policy.
2 Disadvantages:
a   as explained in the chapter dealing with project evaluation, it may be difficult to associate particular R&D expenditure with its attributable revenues on a non-arbitrary basis;
b   as the R&D charge against profits is deferred from its period of incidence to subsequent 'relevant' periods, the initial boosting effect on profit may encourage an over-commitment of cash resources to profits distribution.

1   Advantages:
a   as this method merely covers the charging of expense and
        crediting of revenues in the periods in which they are incurred,
        it avoids the problem of associating costs and revenues inherent
        in the deferral approach;
b   it discourages excessive distribution of profits, particularly at
        times when R&D expenditure is incurred in advance of un-
        certain outcomes, which may themselves require substantial
        funding.
2   Disadvantage:
        unless R&D expenditure is of a recurring nature such that its
        volume does not vary significantly from year to year, then the
        time lag between the incidence of expenditure and attributable
        income may have a disproportionate effect upon short-term
        profitability.

It may be inferred that the balance of preference lies with the 'write-
off' method and this is borne out by Table 10.1 which is taken from
the annual *Survey of Published Accounts* prepared by the Institute of
Chartered Accountants and based on a sample of 300 major British
Companies. The survey notes that the disclosure of R&D expenditure
is improving each year.

TABLE 10.1   Treatment in accounts of R&D expenditure from
a sample of 300 major British companies

	Number of instances 1973/1974	
Assets carried forward in balance sheet		
Fixed assets	2	
Assets neither fixed nor current (deferred expenditure)	1	
Current assets	6	
		9
Expenditure written off		
To profit and loss account (including cases of depreciation of a fixed asset and deferred expenditure	130	
Against reserve or provision	–	
		130
Specific reserves or provisions carried forward		–
		139

There is difficulty in making comparisons between what occurs in practice and what is advocated by accountants who are following accepted principles or conventions. As indicated above, the descriptions contained in published accounts are often ambiguous or do not give enough detail to be able to assess precisely what action has been taken. Some companies write off the expenditure within the year in which it is incurred. Others attempt to assess the future benefits and charge accordingly. Where considerable expenditure is incurred at a particular time, and of an extraordinary nature, then the deferring of expenditure could clearly be appropriate.

Where experience shows that the expenditure incurred year by year tends to be constantly large and stable, or is on the increase, then unless substantial changes are expected in sales revenue, it might be better financially, to write off the expenditure as and when it occurs. Otherwise, the expectation of increased sales revenues from the R&D is never forthcoming, and the company sets itself an impossible task − attempting to write off expenditure against increased sales which are never realised.

There are many difficulties in attempting to lay down standard procedures for dealing with R&D expenditure. Each company's problems and circumstances will require the exercise of judgement in determining how the principles of accounting can be applied. Much more attention should be paid to assessing the likely effect of R&D expenditure in terms of costs, the impact on cash flow and the generation of future sales. Whilst there must be some acknowledgement that the results of R&D are often difficult to forecast, this is not to say that the procedures followed should not be of the type which quickly show when matters are not proceeding according to plan and, therefore, will allow a decision to be made as to how the expenditure should be treated. If the implications are known, then a consistent policy can be adopted regarding the writing off of expenditure, so that the accounts show a true and fair view from one year to another.

10.6   SOME EXAMPLES OF R&D ACCOUNTING TREATMENT

The following is a selection of statements on disclosure of R&D made in annual accounts (or attached reports) in recent years:

1   *The Boots Company Limited*
       Research and development   'Expenditure, other than on

buildings and plant, is charged against profits in the year in which it is incurred.'

2   *Pilkington Brothers Limited*
Research and development   'Revenue and expenditure on research and development is charged against profits of the year in which it is incurred and is not carried forward as an asset to be recouped out of future profits. Capital expenditure on research laboratories, equipment and plant is written off over its expected working life.'

3   *Vickers Limited*
Revised treatment of development expenditure   'In previous years it has been the practice to carry forward to the balance sheet only that part of development expenditure considered to be recoverable from the proceeds of future sales. . . .

   The Directors have now decided to charge against trading profit all development expenditure in the year in which it is incurred. . . .

   Normal research expenditure continues to be charged against trading profit in the year in which it is incurred.'

4   *Fisons Limited*
Development expenditure   'Expenditure incurred in the operation of major new plant during the period between its installation and the achievement of normal operational efficiency and in connection with the establishment of markets for new products, has been carried forward and is being written off over periods considered appropriate.'

10.7   OBJECTIONS TO DISCLOSURE OF R&D ACTIVITY

The research paper, – *Study of Accounting for R&D Expenditure* – discerned the following reasons for companies avoiding or limiting disclosure of R&D activities:

1   As there is no universally acceptable definition of R&D expenditure, information comparison (one of the principal reasons for disclosure) is invalid, or at least unacceptably crude.
2   Disclosure of the amount of expenditure is of itself useless to shareholders and financial analysts, unless it is accompanied by detailed information about projects undertaken and expected profitability.
3   Some manufacturers, particularly in the consumer durable

sector, are unwilling to give information which will help competitors to know when new products are imminent, and which particular fields are being investigated.

In summary then, the treatment of R&D expenditure is an area which through neglect, has resulted in unnecessary confusion and consequent disparity. There is need for an explicit statement on the definition R&D and the requirement for its disclosure − this should be either in statutory form or a recommendation from the accountancy profession.

It is not an easy task as it must resolve the particular problems of:

1 Encompassing the diverse nature of R&D experienced throughout the entire spectrum of industry.
2 Establishing accounting policies which are both consistent with the above constraint, and able to reflect adequately the circumstances of individual companies.

The objective is clear − the impetus required for its attainment not so

10.8 THE AUDITOR'S RESPONSIBILITY

The external auditor has a responsibility to ensure that deferred R&D expenditure is permissible on the grounds that future revenues will be generated. When, as is sometimes the case, there is clearly no hope whatsoever of additional revenues, then the audit report may have to be qualified. Where the amount is material, i.e. significant in relation to overall expenditure or profits, then the audit report might include a note to the effect that the deferred expenditure should have been written off and the profit or loss account would be affected by the specific amount concerned.

11
CASH
MANAGEMENT

11.1   IMPACT OF R&D ON LIQUIDITY

Research and development expenditure can affect the cash flow in a
number of fundamental ways. Unless the possible impact of the policy
being pursued is considered, there is a constant danger of a liquidity
problem and even a financial crisis. As shown earlier, major companies
spend millions of pounds each year and, therefore, even a small
percentage increase can create difficulties by causing a shortage of
cash at a critical time.

The importance of cash forecasting and budgeting is so obvious
that the mechanics may not be operated as swiftly as required to deal
with grave situations. The fact that a company is earning a substantial
profit can give the impression that all is well. Regretfully, as many
boards have discovered, showing satisfactory profitability is no sure
guide to solvency!

The impact on the cash flow will be influenced by the treatment
adopted for the R&D expenditure. Each case should be taken on its
merits and analysed in relation to its effect on the cash for the specific
year. Thus:

Example 1   Commitments entered into in current year for £3 million
over the next 4 years.
Question   When will the work be done and when will payments have to

be made? When there is major structural work, payment may be delaye until specific stages of completion. It is the date when payment is mad not the commitment which determines the cash situation.

Example 2   R&D expenditure spent in current year £2 million, but
               costs deferred to future periods?
Question   Have accounts been settled? If so, £2 million will have to b
met from current finances. However, the deferring of costs will have an
effect on cash flow in future years as shown in Figure 11.1

Profit	£4.0 million
Less Depreciation	£1.0 million
R&D expenditure written off	£0.5 million
NET PROFIT AVAILABLE FOR DISTRIBUTION AND RESERVES	£2.5 million

Figure 11.1   Example

It will be seen that the act of deducting the depreciation and deferre R&D expenditure has the effect of conserving cash resources. However whether amounts are actually available in cash will depend upon the policy which has been pursued throughout the year. In many growing companies, the expenditure will tend to outstrip revenues and, there-fore, the cash resources will be consumed and become stocks, debtors or other short-term assets which earn profit.

11.2   PLANNING AND CONTROL

Corporate objectives should be specified for all major activities includir R&D. The purpose should be to relate expected achievements with costs, including the optimum utilisation of cash resources. The forecast ing of cash should include an examination of a number of important areas:

1   Integration of all functions   The inter-relationship between the various functional activities should be recognised within the forecasts made. An offensive marketing strategy may call for a more positive direction for R&D which, in turn, could lead to a higher rate of spendir

2   Achievement of plans made   Quite often the R&D expenditure is

governed by some important factor such as sales achieved, or profit
earned. If the key factor fails to materialise, there may be need to look
very closely at the level of expenditure on R&D. Where there is a serious
short-fall, steps may have to be taken to cut back on research. Yet this
step should be avoided if at all possible, because it is at this time that
new products and methods may be vital to the improvement of results.
If R&D is to continue at the same rate, fresh finance may have to be
sought.

3   Control of spending   When cash is a limiting factor, there should
be a careful watch kept on the rate of spending. With R&D and capital
expenditure, payments might be scheduled so that they are made at a
time when cash flow is quite good and, conversely, avoided when there
is a seasonal downturn in receipts. Continuing work will obviously
have to be paid for, but there may be a considerable volume which
can be delayed to co-incide with the most advantageous period for
cash resources. Remember, if there is overspending on R&D projects,
some other function may have to suffer with detrimental effects on
the business!

4   Possibility of commercial exploitation   When operating in a highly
competitive market, the availability of liquid resources to exploit
commercial opportunities may be of paramount importance. An important policy issue is to decide how much should be earmarked for
this purpose. Obviously a company cannot afford to have idle resources,
but is may be possible to have cash tied up in short-term investments
which can be realised without difficulty. Where commercial exploitation of a product is imminent, there is much to be said for having a
contingency fund which can be used without delay.

11.2.1   *Viability of projects*

In appraising proposals for R&D work, as explained in Chapter 5, it
will be necessary to consider the timing of cash flows. Indeed, unless
the latter are satisfactory, a project may have to be delayed.
   A careful watch should be kept on expenditure by marking off
payments against commitments. If these get out of step, when large
sums of money are involved, the planned cash flow may be seriously
affected.

11.2.2   *Cash required influences approval of R&D projects*

All decisions to approve or reject R&D projects will be influenced by the amount of finance available. In many companies this will be limited, so there is always a danger that management may be tempted to underestimate the amount required, in order to obtain approval of the project. The existence of a system of cash management which will show up cases where this has happened should act as a powerful deterrent and, when it does happen, will enable appropriate action to be taken at an early stage. Care should be taken to ensure that projects are not 'divided up' to appear to be costing less than is actually the case.

11.2.3 Implications of cash rationing

There are times in most businesses when there is a severe shortage of cash. These may be during a Government 'credit squeeze' or due to expansion of the business coinciding with unfavourable conditions for raising additional loan or equity capital. In such a situation, it will be necessary to ration cash available for financing fixed assets, current assets and R&D expenditure. A restriction on R&D expenditure will probably mean that there will have to be some adjustment to the projects being carried out, giving priority to those which are likely to earn a positive cash flow in the short term, as opposed to those project which are more attractive in the long term. An examination of the fore cast net cash flow profiles of the various projects, as illustrated in Figure 5.3, will quickly show which projects fall into each of these categories. With effective cash management, it should be possible to obtain advance warning of the need for such adjustments. In turn, it should be possible to modify the R&D programme more easily before incipient damage has occurred.

11.2.4 Effect on dividends

Decisions on whether R&D expenditure should be charged against the profits for the year or deferred into future years will affect the profits shown in the accounts as being available for distribution. Thus, in simple form, the entries necessary may be as shown in Figure 11.2.

The profit and loss account shows a profit of £300,000 available for payment of dividends. If these are paid, the bank account will be overdrawn by £250,000 which is unlikely to be an acceptable course of action when funds are low. Writing off the whole or part of the R&D expenditure would have resulted in a more realistic presentation of the cash position. Cash management should ensure that the possible effects of dividends or other major payments are taken into account before the act is authorised. Forward-planning and subsequent monitoring are essential to avoid cash crises and emergency borrowing.

'Cash management' is the term given to describe the systematic approach to all aspects of planning and controlling the financial resources, especially the working capital. It involves:

1   Forecasting cash inflows and outflows.
2   Scheduling commitments so that cash usage is optimised.
3   Converting cash forecasts (probabilities) into cash budgets which represent part of an integrated plan.
4   Monitoring results by comparing actual payments (or periodic amounts) with budgeted payments.
5   Taking action to ensure adequate availability of cash at any time.

The aim is to obtain the optimum use of cash resources without en-dangering the business and, at the same time, to keep idle cash to a minimum. Cash forecasts and budgets are essential together with periodic cash flow reports.

11.4   CASH FORECASTS AND BUDGETS

There are two essential stages for planning and controlling cash resources:

1   Medium to long-term requirements covering the main items of revenue and expenditure (cash forecast);
2   Short-term cash payments and receipts usually for a year and possibly month-by-month (short-term forecast and budget).

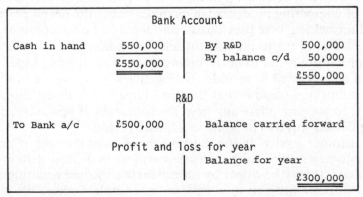

Figure 11.2

For R&D both a forecast and budget will be essential. The distinction between the two is not always clear cut; essentially the forecast is concerned with the *probable* cash position. It covers medium- and long-term requirements, but could also deal with the short period cash flows until the plans have been finalised. Once the latter occurs, the yearly forecast becomes the annual budget being fully integrated with all other functions. However, when the cash flow is uncertain or critical — cash being a limiting factor — a month-by-month analysis will be necessary:

1   Estimating cash inflows and outflows in a short-term cash forecast.
2   Making any adjustments or financing arrangements.
3   Incorporating the finalised cash forecast details into the cash budget.

There will always be need for a close watchfulness, but where the liquidity position is quite adequate there may be no need for short-term forecasts; the cash budget will be made 'firm' for a period of, say, six months and any variances from budgeted figures should be sufficient for taking the necessary steps to avoid any cash shortages. The nature of a cash forecast is explained in the next section.

Some companies produce only one cash budget for the whole company, but where the expenditure of the R&D department is substantial, it will probably be desirable to have a separate cash budget. It may also be desirable to distinguish quite clearly which costs are fixed and which are variable. For an example of a cash budget for the R&D department for a year see Figure 11.3.

In most businesses, new R&D opportunities or requirements arise during the year. Examples of these are suggested new applications for a company's products, increases in the price of raw materials which make recovery from scrap or effluent worthwhile, or increases in the cost of competing products which make viable the development of products which were previously considered to be uneconomic. The budget should try to provide sufficient flexibility for such opportunities or requirements to be accommodated. The items in Figure 11.3 could be extended to include contingencies. However, in this example the assumption made is that the work already scheduled could be varied to accommodate any new developments; if necessary, deferring the planned work to be done in a future period.

'Customer service' in the illustration refers to the cost of providing a day-to-day service to the sales department in dealing with customers' enquiries. It may be offset by miscellaneous income resulting from R&D work on projects now regarded as complete where the income element is no longer being recorded in detail.

CASH BUDGET: 19-- DEPARTMENT: R&D £'000	Jan	Feb	Mar	Apr	May	Jun	Jul	Aug	Sep	Oct	Nov	Dec	Total
Allocated expenditure:													
Project: ABC/100	4	4	4	3	-	-	-	-	-	-	-	-	15
/107	6	4	-	-	-	-	-	-	-	-	-	-	10
/110	7	7	5	3	3	3	3	3	2	-	-	-	36
/111	3	3	2	-	-	-	-	-	-	-	-	-	8
/112	-	10	4	2	2	2	-	-	-	-	-	-	20
/113	-	15	7	5	5	5	5	5	-	-	-	-	47
/114	-	-	-	9	8	8	8	7	7	7	7	7	68
/115	-	-	-	-	-	-	25	15	15	15	15	15	100
Customer service	2	2	2	2	2	2	2	2	2	2	2	2	24
SUB-TOTAL	22	45	24	24	20	20	43	32	26	24	24	24	328
Less recoveries:													
ABC/107	4	3	2	-	-	-	-	-	-	-	-	-	9
/115	-	-	-	-	-	-	-	-	[20]	-	-	[10]	[30]
SUB-TOTAL	4	3	2	-	-	-	-	-	20	-	-	10	39
Net	18	42	22	24	20	20	43	32	6	24	24	14	289
CAPITAL EXPENDITURE	-	-	20	-	1	-	15	-	1	-	-	-	37
Overhead expenses of dept.													
Administrative salaries	5	5	5	5	5	5	6	6	6	6	6	6	66
Accommodation expenses	1	1	8	1	1	8	1	1	8	1	1	8	40
Other expenses	2	2	2	2	2	2	2	2	2	2	2	2	24
SUB-TOTAL	8	8	15	8	8	15	9	9	16	9	9	16	130
TOTAL NET CASH OUTFLOW	26	50	57	32	29	35	67	41	23	33	33	30	456
CUMULATIVE NET CASH OUTFLOW	26	76	133	165	194	229	296	337	360	393	426	456	

Figure 11.3 Cash budget for R&D department. Bold squares indicates differences between Figures 11.3 and 11.4

If this treatment is applied, the cost of providing customer service will be budgeted as part of the overheads of the sales department and charged directly against profits so will not appear on the R&D cash budget.

'Recoveries' refers only to projects where the customer will pay directly for part of all of the R&D costs. Although it will be necessary to measure the recovery of R&D costs included in selling prices in order to confirm that a project has achieved what was originally planned, it would probably be too cumbersome to separate such recovery for cash budgets and cash forecasts.

11.4.1   Comparison with operating budget

The operating budget is concerned with the financial evaluation of the planned activities of a company or a section within it, such as a department. It attempts to show the responsibilities of the Board (company budget) or a specific manager. Sometimes a budget will cover a specific function like marketing or R&D.

Since an operating budget is concerned with activities for a segment of a business, it follows that all *planned* revenue and expenditure for the budget period will be included even though payment is made or received in a different period. This fact emphasises a fundamental difference in the content of the cash budget which includes only cash payments and receipts for a period.

In the conventional cash budget which analyses the cash position month-by-month, no account will be taken of non-cash items such as depreciation or R&D expenditure written off in the specific year. However, in the source and application of funds statement, any amounts written off deferred expenditure will have the effect of increasing cash.

11.4.2   Cash forecast

As indicated earlier, the cash forecast is an estimate of what will happen in the future under the influence of postulated external factors and internal actions, whereas the cash budget represents a plan of action to achieve desired future results. At the time when budgets are prepared a cash forecast and budget will often agree but, subsequently, by the beginning of the financial year, circumstances may have changed Figure 11.4 shows a cash forecast for 19. . prepared in January 19. . for the R&D department whose cash budget is shown in Figure 11.3.

The forecast differs from the budget because it has become clear that:

CASH BUDGET: 19--   DEPARTMENT: R&D   £'000

	Jan	Feb	Mar	Apr	May	Jun	Jul	Aug	Sep	Oct	Nov	Dec	Total
Allocated expenditure:													
Project ABC/100	4	4	4	3	–	–	–	–	–	–	–	–	15
/107	6	4	–	–	–	–	–	–	–	–	–	–	10
/110	7	7	5	3	3	3	3	3	2	–	–	–	36
/111	3	3	2	–	–	–	–	–	–	–	–	–	8
/112		10	4	2	2	2	–	–	–	–	–	–	20
/113		15	7	5	5	5	5	5	–	–	–	–	47
/114				9	8	8	8	7	7	7	7	7	68
/115							25	15	15	15	15	15	100
Customer service	2	2	2	2	2	2	2	2	2	2	2	2	24
SUB-TOTAL	22	45	24	24	20	20	43	32	26	24	24	24	328
Less recoveries:													
ABC/107	4	3	2	–	–	–	–	–	–	–	–	–	9
/115	–	–	–	–	–	–	–	–	–	–	–	–	–
SUB-TOTAL	4	3	2	–	–	–	–	–	–	–	–	–	9
Net	18	42	22	24	20	20	43	32	26	24	24	24	319
CAPITAL EXPENDITURE	–	–	[–]	–	[21]	–	15	–	1	–	–	–	37
Overhead expenses of dept.													
Administrative salaries	5	5	5	5	5	5	6	6	6	6	6	6	66
Accommodation expenses	1	1	8	1	1	8	1	1	8	1	1	8	40
Other expenses	2	2	2	2	2	2	2	2	2	2	2	2	24
SUB-TOTAL	8	8	15	8	8	15	9	9	16	9	9	16	130
TOTAL NET CASH OUTFLOW	26	50	37	32	49	35	67	41	43	33	33	40	486
CUMULATIVE NET CASH OUTFLOW	26	76	113	145	194	229	296	337	380	413	446	486	
BUDGET	26	76	133	165	194	229	296	337	360	393	426	456	

Figure 11.4 Cash forecast for R&D department. Bold squares indicate differences between Figures 11.3 and 11.4

1   Delivery of the capital equipment budgeted to be paid for in
         March will be delayed.
2   Part payment by the customer of the R&D costs on project
         ABC/115 anticipated under 'recoveries' will not be received.

In addition to these changes, there may have to be later modifications
which arise from the need to develop new products or ideas. Whether
these will call for a complete revision of the cash budget depends upon
the significance of the changes in plans. As far as possible every
attempt should be made to keep to the original specification, but
where cash is involved any serious shortage can call for drastic action.
A company without adequate working capital is likely to flounder very
quickly. In the absence of short-term support from financial institution
trading would have to be restricted with a still further deterioration in
the cash position. Research and develop work would also suffer and
stagnation could follow.

11.4.3   Updating cash forecasts and budgets

As indicated earlier, if there are changing circumstances which call for
firm cash management, it will be necessary to produce a new updated
cash forecast at regular intervals, usually monthly, but possibly each
quarter. Moreover, since the cash forecast for the R&D department
will be used in updating the company's cash forecast, the frequency of
the requirement for an updated company's cash forecast will determine how often the R&D cash forecast is produced. Coordination of
the various functions requires that procedures should be time-tabled
and effected to a strict schedule.
    In updating a cash forecast, it is always difficult to distinguish
between the expenditure which has been incurred and the cash which
has been paid out in respect of that expenditure. This is inevitable
in a society which has extensive credit facilities. Some form of estimating may be used to avoid the considerable clerical effort of establishing in each case exactly what has been paid. For example, it may be
considered sufficiently accurate to assume that apart from the costs
of the payroll, all expenses are paid either one or two months after
they are incurred. The extent to which this does not actually happen
can be taken into account in total by adjusting the company's cash
forecast.
    The cash forecast will normally be required in detail for at least
one year ahead so that cash forecasts prepared during the year will
extend beyond the period of the annual budget. An example of the
cash forecast for the R&D department prepared at 1 July 19. . is
shown in Figure 11.5.

CASH FORECAST: July 19-- to June 19--							DEPARTMENT: R&D					£'000
	Jul	Aug	Sep	Oct	Nov	Dec	Jan	Feb	Mar	Apr	May	Jun	Total
Allocated expenditure:													
Project: ABC/110	3	3	2										8
/112	2	–											2
/113	3	5											8
/114	8	8	7	7	7	7	6	3					53
/115	25	14	14	14	14	14	14	8	5				122
/116							3	6	3				12
/117								3	8	8	8	8	35
/118									6	12	12	12	42
/119									–	2	3	3	8
Customer service	2	2	2	2	2	2	2	2	2	2	2	2	24
SUB-TOTAL	43	32	25	23	23	23	25	22	24	24	25	25	314
Less recoveries: ABC/118	–	–	–	–	–	–	–	–	–	–	3	6	9
Net	43	32	25	23	23	23	25	22	24	24	22	19	305
CAPITAL EXPENDITURE	–	–	15	–	–	–	–	–	1	–	–	20	36
Overhead expenses of dept.													
Administrative salaries	6	6	7	6	6	6	6	6	6	6	6	6	73
Accommodation expenses	1	1	8	1	1	8	1	1	8	1	1	8	40
Other expenses	2	2	3	2	2	2	2	2	3	2	2	2	26
SUB-TOTAL	9	9	18	9	9	16	9	9	17	9	9	16	139
TOTAL NET CASH OUTFLOW	52	41	58	32	32	39	34	31	42	33	31	55	480
CUMULATIVE NET CASH OUTFLOW	282	323	381	413	445	484	34	65	107	140	171	226	
BUDGET	296	337	360	393	426	456			110			220	

Figure 11.5 Cash forecast updated at half year

The cash forecast shows the cumulative net cash outflow compared with budget and Figure 11.6 shows the detailed reconciliation between the two figures.

In the example given, budget figures for 19. . are only shown quarterly. The assumption made is that the long-term budgets from which these figures are taken do not analyse the information into periods shorter than a quarter.

11.4.4   Sources of information

The sources of information from which cash forecasts will be prepared and updated will include:

1   Budgets for individual projects.
2   The revenue budget for R&D expenditure.
3   The company's cash forecast or any decisions resulting from a consideration of the cash position which restrict the total amount available for R&D.
4   Creditors' budget – indicating the period of credit to be taken.
5   Project operating statements.
6   Progress reports on projects which indicate changes in timing or in the level of expenditure.

The person preparing or updating cash forecasts will also take into account any other relevant information which becomes available. This may be of the type which will affect either the amount of cash to be spent or due, the timing of the expenditure or its recovery.

11.5   MANAGEMENT ACTION

Management may need to take action on the expected cash flows of the R&D department as shown by the cash forecast (Figure 11.4) for the following reasons:

1   The R&D cash flow is not expected to be in line with budget, most frequently due to over expenditure on one or more projects.
2   The company's cash forecast indicates that due to the cash flows of other functions not being in line with budget, it is necessary to alter cash flows for the R&D function.

Action may be required to reduce or increase the net cash flows of the R&D function. As a large part of the expenditure of R&D often relates to salaries and these represent a fixed cost, it is difficult to

R&D DEPARTMENT

Reconciliation of cumulative cash outflow to 31 December 19--
Forecast with budget, £'000

Cumulative per forecast			484	
Cumulative per budget			456	
Increase			28	

Result from the following:

	Actual to 30/6/--	Forecast to 31/12/--	Total	
Allocated expenditure on:				
Project ABC/107	2	–	2	Overspend
/112	(2)	2	–	
/113	6	(2)	4	Overspend
/114	(3)	1	(2)	Underspend
/115	–	(5)	(5)	Project delayed
Customer service	2	–	2	Overspend in May
	5	(4)	1	
Less recoveries:				
ABC/107	(1)	–	(1)	Increased recovery
/115	–	30	30	No recovery expected
Capital expenditure	4	26	30	Car not bought
	–	(1)	(1)	
Overhead expenses:				
Administrative salaries	–	1	1	See accounts
Accommodation expenses	(1)	–	(1)	
Other expenses	(2)	1	(1)	
	1	27	28	

Figure 11.6 Reconciliation of forecast with budget. (Note: parentheses indicate a reduction in expenditure

quickly increase or decrease this part of the expenditure. Long-term planning and cash forecasting are therefore vitally important in determining in advance whether it is necessary to increase staff by recruitment or to reduce it by natural wastage.

11.5.1 Action to decrease net cash outflows

In the short term, action to decrease the net cash outflows should concentrate on the following:

1 Delaying payments on accounts Obviously it is necessary to consider what capital expenditure can be delayed. It is also important to consider what purchases of material or equipment for each project can be delayed, particularly if some projects are running behind their original planned timetable.

2 Speeding up 'recoveries' and collection of debts It may be necessary to establish that, in determining prorities for the various projects being dealt with by R&D, particular attention should be given to those which will produce a cash inflow in the near future. These will include projects where a customer has agreed to pay part or all of the development costs, particularly if he has agreed or can be persuaded to make progress payments; projects which employ expensive plant and equipment which is to be sold on completion and those which are expected to provide a quick payback.

3 Obtain sub-contract work for which payment will be received Where an opportunity for work can be created, this has the advantage of enabling a company to keep present staff employed without the cost of such employees being borne by the company.

4 Consolidating the financial position A solution may be to find alternative finance for capital expenditure or even for some R&D projects. Instead of incurring capital expenditure for plant and equipment, it may be considered profitable to lease these assets. Alternatively, the capital expenditure may be spread over a longer period by means of a hire purchase agreement. It may be possible to finance an R&D project by making it a joint venture either with a major customer or with the National Research Development Corporation, but this is not likely to improve the cash flows in the short-term, due to the time it would take to complete an agreement on such a venture.

Many companies and individuals forget that one of the most important sources of cash for a company is its profits. Any action of the

R&D department, therefore, which can quickly enable the company
to improve its profits, should help the cash position of the company.
An example of this might be assisting a major customer with problems
he is encountering in using a new product supplied by the company
(assuming payments can be negotiated).

11.5.2   Action to increase net cash outflows

If the need to take such action arises, attention will be directed to
bringing forward the incurring of expenditure, particularly on projects
with a high material and equipment content or on capital expenditure.
In addition, the possibility of having R&D work done outside the
company on a sub-contract basis should be considered. As will be
appreciated, the need for action to increase cash outflows arises very
infrequently. This is because most companies are restricted by shortage
of cash to finance expansion or simply to finance the increase in
value of stocks, debtors and fixed assets as a result of the effects of
inflation. It is this need for an ever-increasing amount of cash to continue the operations of the company, which makes cash management
of all activities of the company including R&D, so vitally important.

12
COST ACCOUNTING FOR R&D

12.1 THE COST ACCOUNTING SYSTEM

There are different approaches suggested for controlling the R&D
function. In earlier chapters, reference was made to using budgetary
control, and this approach is to be recommended. Budgets can be
established for the function as a whole and then for individual budget
centres.

Individual budgets might be compiled for each project, which
would certainly apply for development work and applied research..

For most situations, and particularly in the earliest stages of
development of a system, it will be necessary to design procedures for
estimating the actual cost of each project. Subsequently, with experience, the accounting system can incorporate budgeted costs.
Eventually standard costs can be introduced to show in detail the
expected costs for individual projects.

12.2 CHARGING COSTS TO PROJECTS

In designing a costing system, precise requirements will be determined
by the nature of the business and the R&D work carried out. As a
first step, it will be necessary to determine the major classification

under which the costs are to be accumulated. As shown earlier, the
major categories are as follows:

1   Basic research.
2   Applied research.
3   Development work.

These would then be sub-divided according to the nature of the
operations. The purpose would be to show the accumulation of costs
relating to each major category. Thus for example:
1   *Basic research*
     a   Division A.
     b   Division B.
Where the work can be sub-divided within each division, this would
be done.

2   *Applied research*
     a   Research on Product XY;
     b   Research on Product RO;
     c   Research on Product PX.
These would be further broken down on the basis of project numbers.
Precisely how far this could be done would depend whether an individual product could be treated separately in accumulating the
costs.

3   *Development Work* which would be analysed in a similar fashion
     to the applied research. Further possible categories would be:
     a   Customer's special work.
     b   Fixed assets produced for use in the company.
This approach will show the major items of expenditure in relation to
the nature of the work. Eventually the costs could be related to the
benefits obtained, and used for assessing the effectiveness of the
R&D function.

12.3   ACCOUNTING ENTRIES

If all costs are to be covered in a fully integrated accounting system,
control accounts would be opened in the integrated ledger. In companies where a separate cost ledger is kept, apart from the financial
records, the accounts would be kept in that ledger. When incurred,
the costs would be posted month by month, to appropriate control
accounts. In the simplest case, there would be two accounts, one for
research and one for development. Actual costs would be debited to
these accounts and then transferred to detailed subsidiary accounts
according to the information built up on the costs sheets in the

Costing Department (described later). A flow chart of the accounting procedures is shown in Figure 12.1. The debits on the control account would come from the bank account or *via* a purchase ledger in the case of the integrated ledger, or a special cost control account if a cost ledger is maintained. These costs would then be transferred at the end of each month into accounts covering each major activity area. This flow chart deliberately simplifies the procedures, the assumption being that all expenditure will be transferred to basic research, and applied research accounts from the research control account, and to the fixed assets and product development accounts from the development control account. In turn, those four accounts would be closed by transfer to either *cost of sales* or *profit and loss account,* or *asset accounts,* the latter to appear on the balance sheet.

In practice, decision must be made as to which items are to be written off and when, and balances may be carried forward from one month to another until a decision is made. As an expediency, the amount to be written off is often decided after the profit is known. However this practice is not advocated. The purpose of cost accounting is to show the true situation on costs and not to manipulate them to suit specific circumstances. 'Consistency', that much laboured word in accountancy, would not be present if charges were varied to adjust the profit for a particular period.

Where a charge is made to a customer, the appropriate cost account would be credited and the customer's account debited. For example, if laboratory tests were carried out, the applied research account might be credited, thus charging the customer with the appropriate fee, which would have the effect of reducing the charge remaining for R&D. The question of what is a realistic charge should also be considered. This applies whether selling to an outside customer or within the company; with the latter, some form of transfer pricing policy would have to be adopted.

12.3.1 The coding system

If costs are to be traced to each project or other classification, then a suitable code system must be considered. This should be flexible enough to allow all items of expense to be included, and at the same time, it should be fully understood by the personnel concerned. In addition, it must fit in with the accounting system, whether this is a hand-posted, mechanical, or computer system.

In designing an accounts code, attention should be paid to all activity areas and these would be linked with a fully comprehensive coding system. The appropriate section for research and development is shown in Table 12.1. This breakdown should indicate how the

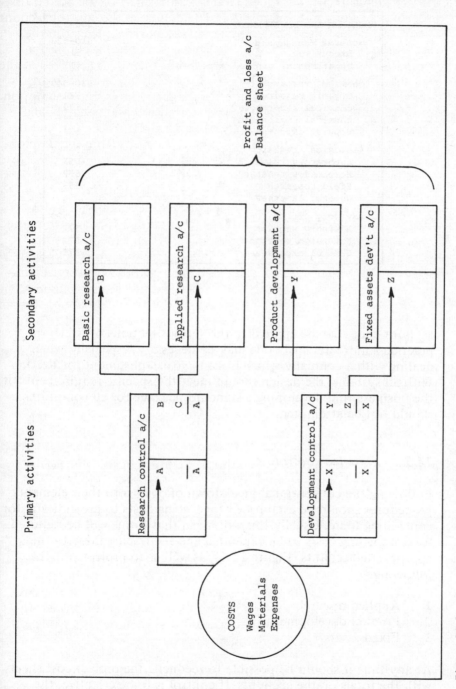

Figure 12.1 Flow diagram of major F&D cost accounts

TABLE 12.1

RESEARCH AND DEVELOPMENT	500–599
General Management	510–529
Executive	511
Departmental general expenses	512
Chemical research	530–549
Organic research	531
Chemical laboratory	532
Chemical engineering	533
General expenses	534
Biological research	550–569
Laboratory research	551
Herbicides research	552
Field research	553
General expenses	554
Advisory Office	570–599
Advisory section	571
Extension section	572
General expenses	573

account codes can be applied to the various sections of R&D. In practice a more detailed code may be necessary, especially when dealing with a company which has a large establishment for R&D. With all systems, the design should meet the specific requirements of the business, and developing a standard package for all conditions should not be attempted.

12.3.2 Detailed control

Following the conventional breakdown of costs into their elements, procedures should be established for tracing costs to projects and for controlling them. Usually this will mean that forms will be required for authorising costs to be expended and for tracing these to the appropriate accounts (Figure 12.1), as well as to projects for the following:

1   Applied research.
2   Product development.
3   Fixed assets.

At any time it should be possible to reconcile the project cost sheets with the totals on the accounts. If control is to be effective, the posting should be made as quickly as possible. The determining

factor should be the time when the figures are available and the 181
degree of control which can be exercised. For some costs, daily
recording may be necessary, but with others, such as general overheads, a monthly charge may suffice. However, much depends upon
the system and the method used for absorbing overhead costs.

Once a project is approved, a job cost sheet should be opened. As
work proceeds, the costs are traced to the project using the authorisation forms such as:

1   *For direct materials*
    a   *Purchase order* and *purchase invoice* for outside suppliers.
    b   *Material requisitions* for any materials issued from stores.
    c   *Material transfer notes* for movements between projects.
    d   *Material return notes* for items returned to the stores
        because they are not required.

These should be authorised by the manager responsible for the department or section. What is important is for a watch to be kept on
usage, particularly when expensive materials are being used. If charging
out the costs to a customer, it will be essential to keep within the
agreed commitment or he may refuse to pay.

When a sophisticated system of control is possible, with direct
materials being capable of exact predetermination, an Excess Material
Requisition may be used. This is a special requisition in a distinctive
colour which authorises quantities in excess of those budgeted. Its
main advantage lies in the fact that attention is being drawn to the
additional requirement before it is actually authorised. Because of
the nature of R&D work, in many establishments there will be limited
application in this approach. Often a material cost is estimated, but
there is no way of knowing its precise composition until the research
is being done.

Where the R&D department has a number of projects in progress
at any one time, it may be desirable to use some form of material
issues abstract. This enables totals to be accumulated by job number,
thus giving figures for posting at the end of each month. The procedure eliminates the need for direct posting from material requisitions and avoids over-burdening job cost sheets. Grand totals can be
used for posting to ledgers, thereby facilitating the reconciliation of
figures for the various control accounts. Even with a computer
system, this form of breakdown may be desirable, and could be
included in the programme. A typical form for summarising issues
is shown in Figure 12.2. This would be adopted to suit the specific
needs.

2   *For labour costs*   The main requirement for labour cost control

MATERIAL ISSUES ANALYSIS FORM																		

Period: _____   No. _____

Ref	Total amount		R&D project numbers															

Figure 12.2 Material issues analysis form

is the correct classification of the work into 'direct' and 'indirect' followed by the use of procedures and records which enable accurate tracing of costs to be made. The *direct costs* are the salaries and wages of research workers who are engaged on projects. Each week a time sheet would be approved by the head of department, thus showing how each individual has been occupied. The time sheets could then be used for direct postings to job cost sheets, or a wages and salaries abstract may be used (see Figure 12.3). Again, as with materials, the totals would be posted to job cost sheets for projects as well as to ledger accounts.

The *indirect labour costs* would represent all the general work in the R&D department. Examples are:

General maintenance labour.
Clerical and secretarial assistance.
Supervision of projects (this may be treated as 'direct' in appropriate circumstances).
Holiday and sickness pay.

The precise classification will depend upon the size and type of

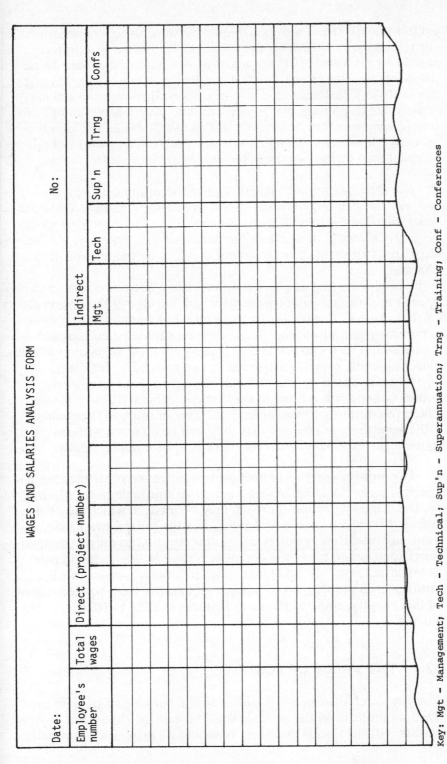

Key: Mgt – Management; Tech – Technical; Sup'n – Superannuation; Trng – Training; Conf – Conferences

Figure 12.3 Wages and salaries analysis form

establishment. It will also be affected by the costing system available for tracing costs. Whenever possible, a direct charge to a project should be preferred. If the accounting is accurate, there can be no disputing the charge and this fact can be important when charging the costs to a customer on a cost-plus basis. However, the tracing of some costs to projects can be onerous, and even when accomplished, would leave much to be desired. In this case, treating the labour cost as an overhead is likely to be more acceptable. The wages and salaries abstract may include columns for analysing these indirect costs.

3 For direct expenses Where some form of job costing is employed, the charging of direct expenses becomes feasible. These are costs incurred for providing special services or facilities for a specific project. Generally these are in the nature of indirect costs, but because they are attributable to one project they can be treated as a direct charge.

Examples are hire of plant and machinery, preparation of drawings, special tooling and any other costs which are clearly the responsibility of that project. The tracing of these direct charges leads to a more accurate system of costing and, therefore, should be encouraged. There would be no justification for charging these costs to overheads, thus burdening projects which had no responsibility for them.

The costs would be traced from invoices or from inter-works orders (when a job is done in another department). Care must be taken to ensure that these special costs are authorised in advance. Otherwise there is a danger that they will be incurred without prior knowledge, especially when the work is to be done internally.

4 For indirect costs Indirect costs which cannot be traced to a specific project, can be apportioned on an equitable basis. Alternatively, the marginal costing approach may be used, in which case only direct costs of a project are charged, and the general overhead costs kept separate. Here, a policy decision is required to determine the most appropriate type of accounting system to use, as it will probably affect not only R&D, but other functions as well. This is a controversial problem on which a great deal has been written. Later in this chapter, some of the main features relating to R&D are considered.

12.4   THE VALUE OF COSTING

Many research managers will object to the booking of time on individual projects on the grounds that it is not the time spent that counts, but the results obtained. It should be recognised that details

1   To ascertain what is being done by each person in R&D.
2   As a guide to the cost incurred to date and to see whether the plans made are being achieved.
3   As a basis for assessing the benefits from each project.
4   For planning manpower and other requirements.
5   To show the R&D managers and personnel that money spent must be justified, and there is a limit to how much cost can be incurred each year — in total and for individual projects.

Having recognised the need for cost control, it is necessary to recognise that overall control can bring about undesirable effects. If a research worker must show how he has spent every fraction of an hour, then he may feel the task is meaningless and frustrating. However, because of the size of manpower costs in many R&D departments, it is necessary to show how the time has been spent. It is worth noting in this respect, that labour costs can be as much as 75 per cent of total R&D expenditure. Is it credible, therefore, to argue that strict control should be confined to materials and other costs when they represent a mere quarter of the total amount spent?

In determining the *detail* required, some form of compromise will be necessary to account for the time spent. First, it should be recognised that scientists and other research personnel may spend some considerable time in attending seminars and conferences, as well as carrying out background research on the problems being encountered. The incidence of such activities is likely to vary between one period and another. A scientist may attend a one week conference in one month, but be fully occupied with specific projects for the whole of the next month. Control must therefore be linked with feasibility or there is a danger that the R&D will suffer.

In some companies a scientist is asked to complete a two weekly time-sheet showing the projects on which he is working. If the time is recorded, some managers believe that any balancing should be done by the accounts department, and if there are shortfalls in the figures, then the assumption is that such time is spent on general research or other activity, which cannot be booked to a project. Whilst this approach relieves the research person from figure work, it is doubtful whether this approach would be acceptable to all companies. Many scientists are also mathematicians, and therefore time allocation should not be an insuperable problem!

In achieving the required flexibility, but at the same time ensuring that the time spent is effective, there is much to be said for stipulating an activity percentage which is made known to the research personnel. For example, it might be feasible to stipulate that not less than 80 per cent of the total time should be booked to projects, or other approved research and development activities, the remaining 20 per cent would cover on average, any educational activities, such as attending courses and seminars. However, a 20 per cent variation is a considerable figure and if applied generally, would remove all realistic control from a system. The educational needs of individuals will tend to vary, so any attempt to standardise would serve no useful purpose. A more realistic approach is to budget for each person and then to compare with actual activities in terms of days and external costs. This means that the budgeted percentage used may be 10 per cent one month; 20 per cent the next month, and then *nil* for the following. Against this approach is the fact that courses and conferences on new discoveries may be arranged at fairly short notice with the result that they cannot be included in plans which are made months in advance.

Turning to *material control,* it should be clear that any expenditure incurred, or any issues from stores should have been included in the budgets for the year; in other words, there should be prior approval of the required expenditure. There would also be clearly defined levels of expenditure, and a clear indication of the managers who are authorised to sanction each one. When material requisitions, or other authorisation forms are completed, these would be approved by the managers with the necessary authority. With small items, such as the issue of sundry supplies, some block bookings may be made and charged to a project, or, alternatively, these may be treated as indirect costs.

The remaining area of control covers the *indirect costs*: R&D overhead or expenses. These are expenses which cannot be identified with a specific project or research activity. They include departmental administration, building costs, maintenance, depreciation and the provision of such facilities as information and library services. They would extend to the preparation of papers and their presentation at seminars and courses, both externally and within a company. In the latter case, payment may be received from an external body, which can be used to offset the general overhead costs.

12.5   MARGINAL OR ABSORPTION COSTING?

If the marginal costing approach is adopted, these indirect costs would not be charged to projects. There is, however, a problem in adopting this method, for unless costs are charged to a project they would not be recoverable in the price charged to outside customers such as government departments. For this reason, there may be many cases where a charge must be made to cover the indirect costs. However, this is an oversimplification. The question to resolve is whether

absorption costing or marginal costing produces the more acceptable
cost figures. Any method selected should be capable of consistent
application under all circumstances; otherwise, decisions made will
not be based on facts presented in a manner which shows relevance
to the problems on hand. A more positive approach is to ask which
are the *relevant costs,* not whether to use absorption or marginal
costing.

12.5.1 Advantages and limitations

Arguments *in favour* of using marginal costing are as follows:

1   Since the R&D services are already committed, the fixed costs
    have no relevance in determining the cost of a specific project.
2   Pricing of R&D services can be much more realistic when based
    on marginal cost plus a realistic contribution. This approach
    recognises that market forces not costs incurred determine the
    price obtainable at a particular time. Fluctuations due to
    variations in the amount of work done are not affected by the
    amount of fixed overhead applied.
3   The methods of apportioning fixed costs are so arbitrary that
    no useful purpose is served, either for decision making, for con-
    trolling or for establishing any causal relationships between the
    costs incurred and the benefits produced. Accordingly, it is
    argued, manipulating the costs in this way can serve no useful
    purpose.

In *favour of* adopting absorption costing for R&D, the following
arguments may be advanced:

1   Where the activities use different amounts of services which incur
    fixed costs, unless some form of apportionment is attempted, a
    true cost cannot be obtained.
2   With a project the marginal costs may be a relatively small pro-
    portion of the total, and therefore to produce realistic costs it is
    necessary to consider all the services provided.
3   There may be difficulty in justifying charges for R&D services
    when most of the costs have been omitted on the grounds that
    these are not relevant to specific projects.

   These arguments for and against marginal costing are now quite
familiar to most accountants. What is of vital importance is that there
should be an attitude of mind which recognises the important costs
for planning and decision making, as well as for other purposes.

Flexibility should be sought whilst at the same time giving full recognition that for some purposes some idea of total costs will be essential.

What is often lacking in a costing system is an appreciation of how much control can be exercised over the overhead costs which are charged to individual projects. This may be the cause of many problems encountered when trying to justify these charges. If a research manager is told that he cannot control depreciation or the rent of the building which he uses, then he is unlikely to be impressed when told that he has incurred charges for these items. This question of responsibility is a major consideration when setting up a control system.

Different attempts have been made to show how the responsibility for indirect costs can be traced to the R&D function. A careful study of the usage of the services by different departments or sections within R&D can do much to indicate which parts are responsible for the costs incurred. This approach requires careful study and analysis over a period of time, and accordingly takes longer to apply than the square metres, capital values of assets, and similar measures. Nonetheless, some feel the additional effort worthwhile and even use two or three different overhead rates to charge out on the basis of actual or potential usage.

When looking at a system of control for R&D, it must be remembered that if taken too far, the administrative inconvenience and cost can well outweigh the benefits received. Accordingly, a compromise may be better, by getting realistic costs for each project, assessing the value of these in terms of future revenues, and applying realistic measures to indicate whether a project should continue or not. If these requirements are covered, then it may be unnecessary to introduce additional refinements such as multiple overhead rates for absorbing the R&D costs.

12.6   ESTABLISHING A PRICING POLICY

As indicated earlier, because of the diverse nature of R&D operations, costs are dealt with in a variety of ways. Some will be written off in the year in question, others will be charged to customers, and those incurred on fixed assets will be capitalised. Because of the complexity of the situation, it may be difficult to pin-point responsibilities, and yet for effective control this must be achieved.

In establishing a control system there is some merit in dividing the business into responsibility centres and then making these requisition R&D work for their needs. The responsibility centre, whether a separate division, or company, or other operating unit, is treated as a 'customer' of the R&D department. In this situation, realistic transfer prices must be set as a basis for charging user departments with an equitable fee for the services provided.

The ideal aim is to achieve transfer prices which enable full recovery of total R&D costs, and if policy dictates, a fair 'profit'. Generally the charge will be based on the actual costs incurred on the projects, which presents little or no difficulty when considering the direct charges for labour, materials, and supplies which relate to specific projects. Where a problem may arise, is with charging out indirect expenses. With the latter, the methods employed are often rather arbitrary, and may cast doubt on the true costs of the projects.

This problem is also linked with the selection of research projects, which if judged in terms of expected profitability, then the costs must be known. Yet what are the costs when considering the administrative and building charges and the R&D facilities? A decision has already been made to incur these costs which have to be met, whether or not any projects have been requisitioned by customer departments.

A theoretical approach to the charging out of indirect costs can be to make an estimate of what could be earned from the resources, if the work was charged out to an external customer. But even this method is not fool-proof because prices obtained externally are not necessarily related to the costs incurred.

The normal practical approach to the absorption of the indirect cost of projects, is to charge out on the basis of time spent by research workers, which is really the 'percentage-on-direct-labour' method, often used for absorbing production overhead costs.

This approach will require an assessment of the total time available within the R&D department, divided on the basis of potential usage by the customer departments. Once these figures are agreed, then the unit charge for indirect costs can be computed.

This method can be used for assessing whether a project will be profitable. The R&D service would be charged to the user department which would hope to make a profit on the project. In arriving at a transfer price, the R&D department should charge on a realistic basis to cover its costs. There may also be a strong case for charging an additional amount to cover the basic research which cannot be charged out. In addition, there could be justification for having a profit figure to be used as a measure of the performance of the R&D function.

The actual cost of projects would follow similar lines. There is the collection of actual direct costs, followed by absorption of indirect costs, using a suitable basis such as a percentage on direct labour

For control purposes, it is necessary to compare the costs under each major category against budgets or forecasts, and then extract variances which can be examined and analysed to see whether gains are being made, by introducing new methods or other benefits.

13
SYSTEM DESIGN FOR R&D

13.1   THE NEED FOR PROCEDURES

If the R&D function is to operate efficiently there should be planned procedures covering such matters as:

1   The appropriate organisation for R&D including facilities for the personnel required.
2   Evaluation of proposals for research projects.
3   The allocation of priorities including the rationing of funds between the various functions.
4   The control of overall progress, and the progress and expenditure on individual projects.

All these are vital if optimum results are to be obtained. The major problem is to formalise the procedures so that benefits can be maximised without restricting the work of the R&D personnel.

The procedures should be determined after a study is made of the requirements of the particular company. This should be done against the background of a corporate plan which covers the company's total activities; there should be no question of looking at R&D in isolation. Integration is the essential requirement, viewing all functional activities within the framework of a corporate plan.

In Chapter 4 an outline relates R&D activity to the corporate objectives. When designing procedures which are interlocked into a system, there should be an understanding of the overall corporate objectives, as well as those related to R&D.

When looking at the R&D objectives with reference to planning, it may be useful to adopt the 'relevance tree' approach. This includes the use of a chart or diagram which shows the step-by-step approach required to achieve the main objectives; it consists of a breakdown of the objectives into sub-objectives or, simply, the main steps required as far as can be seen to achieve the necessary goals.

A relevance tree is therefore a diagrammatic representation of an area or areas to be covered by the R&D programme. It is broken down into a number of horizontal levels or steps. The top representing the main objective, and the lower levels, the natural steps required. An alternative approach is to break down the overall company objectives into product groups, or other convenient groupings such as separate companies or divisions.

The advantages claimed for this approach are that:

1   An attempt is made to define corporate objectives in a positive and constructive manner.
2   Having defined the corporate objectives it is possible to indicate the main R&D objectives.
3   There is a discipline imposed on all R&D personnel, who must define what they are attempting to achieve.
4   The relevance tree shows the essential facts only, and allows managers to see the salient points.
5   Any projects or proposals which do not fit into the corporate objectives can be identified, deferred, or disregarded.
6   R&D staff can see what they are trying to achieve and can work with particular goals in mind, thus adopting a 'Management by Objectives' approach.
7   Where there are alternative courses of action, these can be listed, and the constraints or limitations discussed, with a view to arriving at an optimum solution. (In effect this is the 'decision tree').

This approach can be adapted to suit any company. The detail can be varied to meet specific requirements, and initially the relevance trees can concentrate on the essential stages, possibly on the quality of product or service, and then subsequently breaking down on further relevance trees, the quantities in terms of cost, manpower, facilities and the time scale.

An illustration of a relevance tree is given in Figure 13.1, but this is a simplified version. It is assumed that the insulation of rooms is not within the orbit of the corporate objectives and attention is concentrated on improving the room thermostats. A further assumption is that the form of heating used, including the power available, such as boilers, is adequate. Accordingly, the whole of the relevance tree looks at the objectives and stages concerned in improving room thermostats.

13.1.2   An alternative approach

Instead of looking at a specific problem, it is possible to produce a relevance tree which outlines the main stages in the overall R&D objectives. This means that at the top of the chart the main objective is stated, as shown in Figure 13.2. The main purpose is to identify, develop and recommend new technologies and equipment for a computer specialising in telecommunications systems.

The company in question supplies equipment to customers and, therefore, the R&D function covers three main areas:

1   Developing enhanced production processes for existing systems.
2   Improving and extending the range of systems which are now available.
3   Exploring new concepts and developments.

In the illustration the second objective is broken down into stages which finally emerge as an individual R&D project. As will be apparent from this description, though somewhat simplified, the purpose is to present stages in a simple manner, so that managers can appreciate what they are trying to achieve, and how it is to be done.

13.2   ESTABLISHING PERFORMANCE INDICATORS

As this stage it would be useful to consider how far the R&D objectives can be evaluated in financial terms. In other words, to what extent can each proposal be justified?

If each project can be separated in terms of cost and benefits, such as increased sales revenues, then the feasible approach may be to evaluate each one in terms of expected profit. In many cases this approach may be impracticable, especially when the overall company objectives are so integrated that they do not fall naturally into separate projects. In these circumstances the performance indicator may have to be some form of overall measure, such as return on capital em-

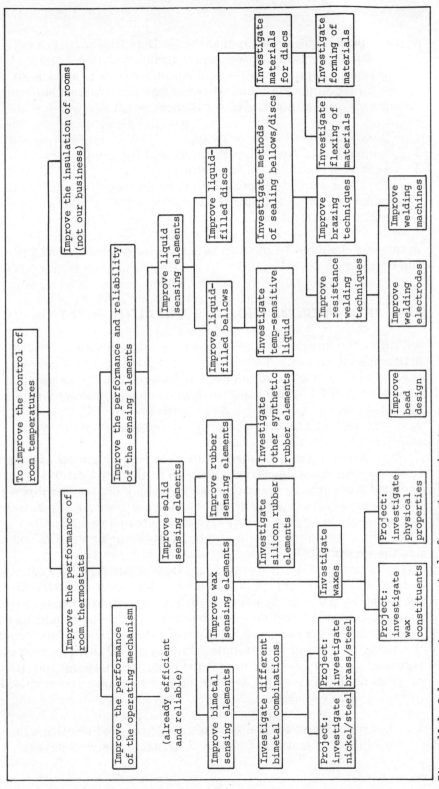

Figure 13.1 Relevance tree – control of room temperatures

ployed, the assumption being that the R&D expenditure is to be capitalised and written off over future accounting periods.

This general approach to the problem should not be used as an excuse for ignoring detail, and wherever possible, there should be preliminary estimates prepared for the following:

1   Detailed costs suitably analysed.
2   Time required for each major stage and for completion.
3   Technical feasibility of each project.
4   Expected benefits where they can be separately identified, and evaluating projects under such headings as 'most likely', 'probable' and 'least likely'.

In this way it should be possible to see the range of expected costs and revenues.

13.3   INITIATION OF PROJECTS AND AUTHORISATION

Within a company it should be possible to see at any time the present deficiencies in technical knowledge, or the possible new areas of development. These requirements may be apparent by having a periodic report from functional managers, such as production and marketing, which indicates areas for development. Additional relevance trees may be used to show what developments are required, and the stage reached for each one.

New discoveries may be made within the R&D department, either from the basic research carried out, or as further applications become apparent from applied research. Alternatively, ideas may be thrown up from other departments in the company, or from totally outside the company, in respect of new inventions created in different fields. Both type of project should be approved in a formal manner, and the system must provide the necessary procedures.

The initiation of projects may stem from a variety of sources, such as the R&D department, the company as a whole, or the external environment. Even simple sources, such as suggestion schemes, may produce ideas which should be followed up. The broad principles will apply whatever the source and it is possible to see from a flow chart the process of how project initiation, appraisal and authorisation can take place. Figure 13.3 summarises the stages in establishing an R&D programme. The first step, 'Areas of Project Initiation', comprises the following main elements:

1   Specification of R&D objectives, strategies, and priorities, including examination of technical strengths and weaknesses.

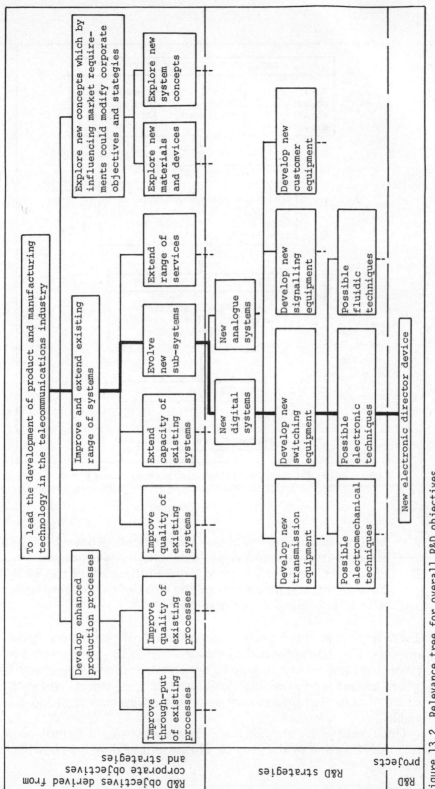

Figure 13.2 Relevance tree for overall R&D objectives

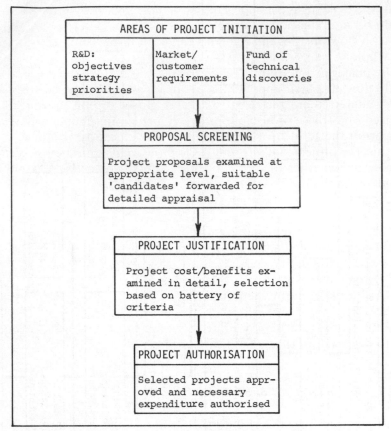

Figure 13.3 Project initiation and authorisation

2   Analysis of consumer and user requirements, from reports pre-
    pared by the marketing department and from customers.
3   The fund of technical discoveries from the work of the R&D
    department, and possibly from the work of other companies,
    or from government departments.

These three elements represent the initiation, or starting point, for
projects. The next stage is the consideration of the preliminary proposals for projects, which may be done at departmental level or,
where an idea seems feasible, consideration by a projects committee
to sanction further preliminary work to see whether the proposal is
viable.

   Once preliminary clearance is given the next step is to look for a
fuller justification of the project. This would be done by showing in

detail the expected cost and benefits as indicated in Chapter 5. Next would be an evaluation of the project, showing its likely profitability and cash flow profile, and its impact in both respects, on the company as a whole.

The managers or committee authorised to sanction the project would now give their approval to go ahead; alternatively, the project may be deferred or even rejected. This might be on the grounds of changed objectives, or because of overriding commitments which will not permit the additional expenditure. It should be ascertained whether the project fits into the R&D programme and the one-year budget, and whether the project can start, and when each stage would be finished.

In summary form, the main stages are as follows:

1   Preparation of a proposal outlining the project.
2   A more detailed analysis of the project in terms of costs and
     expected benefits.
3   Overall approval of the project.
4   Authorisation of expenditure.

Once the work is started it will be necessary to control the plans made and to keep within the expenditure limits.

13.3.1   Procedures for authorisation

The procedures for authorising expenditure should be clearly laid down to avoid any misunderstanding. How this should be done depends upon the type of company, the size of the operation and the accounting system employed. However, as a starting point it is possible to break projects into a number of categories:

1   Major projects which are likely to affect a business as a whole
Major projects are often defined in terms of the expenditure to be incurred, e.g. £20,000 or above. This is not however, the only guide and much will depend upon the nature of a project and whether it should receive consideration at board level. A major project should fit in with the established pattern of corporate objectives, and so avoid conflict between what the company is trying to achieve, and what is being done by the R&D department.

2   Small- to medium-sized projects   Again a limit would be stipulated, say, below £20,000. These should be authorised by the director of research and development and the financial director, or there may be a similar arrangement covering the essential requirements, that anything authorised should be within the company's means, and not be in conflict with the R&D objectives.

3 Minor projects or work contracted by customers   The amount for each would be small, and possibly not exceed say, £200. They would be reported to the director of research and development, so that he is aware of what is happening. When the work is carried out for a customer, there should be normal customer liaison, either by the R&D department, or by the marketing manager. The customer must agree in writing that he will pay for the work being done before it is carried out.

13.3.2   Preparation of proposals for major projects

A more detailed approach is necessary for major projects than for those in the other two categories. However, with major projects, some modification may be necessary when the amount of finance is small. As already indicated there will be a preliminary proposal followed by justification and then evaluation.

The preliminary proposal would be prepared by the research worker or technical manager, who wishes to pursue the research or development outlined in his proposal. A special form may be used for this purpose which would describe the nature of the work, its objectives and a broad statement of its likely benefits. The director of research and development would give it his approval, so that preparation of a full project justification could then start.

The project justification would set out in detail, on a suitable form, all facts required to show why the project should be approved. Possible features are:

1   The objectives.
2   The method proposed, the technical background and the probability of success.
3   The proposed timing of the project, dividing it into the main stages.
4   The resources required to carry out the work.
5   Whether the work is to be done within the company and who is to be responsible, or whether an outside contract is to be awarded.
6   The estimated cost of the project.
7   The inter-relationships which exist between the proposed project and any other existing or proposed projects.
8   The benefits expected in terms of sales revenues, reduced costs, or other performance indicators.

9   A cash flow profile possible on a discounted cash flow (DCF)
    basis.
10 The urgency of the project so that the order of priorities can be
    established.

Once these facts have been collected, the project evaluation stage can
be tackled. This means checking the details of the project and looking
more deeply into the statements made on the project justification
form. Once the facts are validated, a better assessment of the order of
priorities can be obtained. Important matters to be checked are as
follows:

1   Ensure that the objectives stated are still relevant, and there are
    no recent changes which will alter the position.
2   Verify the independence of a project from others in operation,
    or proposed for the future.
3   Check the accuracy of the costs and benefits given in the
    authorisation form.
4   Assess the manpower requirements for the new project.

   A project may be desirable, but may still have to be deferred because of higher priorities. Accordingly all relevant facts must be
considered in deciding whether the current project fits into the
relevance tree. In addition, the expected rate of return should be
checked to ensure that it complies with what has been laid down by
the board. Where it is not feasible to stipulate a rate of return, then
the impact on overall profitability may be determined, or alternatively
some form of cost analysis should be done, this assessing the project
in terms of cost reduction on the common good of the company and
its employees.
   Although each project should be examined for its priority. In this
particular time, there is little merit in classifying projects under type,
and thereby automatically giving them an order of priority. For
example, if a general system of priority ranking is followed, all
projects within a certain category could be given top prioroty. In this
case, there may be a tendency for R&D personnel to request authorisation on those projects, even though there are no facilities for
carrying them out. For many companies therefore looking at each
project separately is perhaps a better plan. The importance of
different types of work change from time to time, and the suggested
approach will ensure the desired flexibility.

Once the evaluation stage is complete, the project justification form can be finalised and submitted to the director of research and development for approval, which would be given only on the understanding that expenditure should be limited to that necessary for the initial stage of the project. There should also be a statement of when the work can commence, thus allowing the impact of the expenditure to be calculated in terms of cash flow.

As the work proceeds, the position of the project should be reviewed, and each subsequent stage approved before proceeding further. If there is a change in circumstances, a project may have to be modified.

13.3.4   Dealing with minor and contracted R&D work

As already stated above, the detailed proposals would only apply to major projects. With full time activities of a routine nature a simplified set of procedures would be followed. Alternatively, a total budget figure would be given for minor projects and provided the R&D department works within the figure, there should be no problem. Precisely how this should be dealt with depends upon the accounting system, but there is considerable merit in keeping the procedures as simple as possible. However, the purpose of the procedure should be the main consideration and this will affect the control periods adopted. For many costs a monthly posting may be adequate, but where figures are significant, daily or weekly totals may be necessary.

13.4   FORMULATION AND SUBMISSION OF THE R&D PROGRAMME

Reference has already been made in earlier chapters to the formulation of an R&D programme. Here it is necessary to look at this aspect with particular reference to the design of a suitable system.

The R&D policy and strategy would cover a period of, say, five years, suitably analysed into the types of projects envisaged. These might be as indicated earlier under Section 13.3.2. Alternatively or additionally, the work can be divided according to the types of the research, such as basic or applied, and development work.

The first year of the five-year programme would then be represented in terms of the annual budget, thus linking the R&D corporate objectives with the next current year's activities.

The R&D programme would be submitted at various stages of its development to the director of research and development. However, the main annual presentation would be made about two months before the end of the financial year. This would show what had been agreed in terms of individual projects, as well as a budget amount for minor projects.

Where revision of the R&D programme is necessary, this would be done so that the changes could be implemented and incorporated in the annual budget. Circumstances which might call for a revision are as follows:

1   A major project is discontinued because the benefits originally expected are not forthcoming.
2   New inventions or significant developments require the R&D objectives to be revised.
3   Considerable urgency for a new product to be introduced.

In these circumstances the revision should be carried out with interruption of the R&D programme as a whole. Moreover the abandonment of a project or the introduction of a new project, should be carried out in such a way that the R&D programme is not thrown out of balance.

13.5   ORGANISATION FOR PROJECT CONTROL

Steps should be taken to ensure there is an adequate organisation to look at submissions and ensure that any abortive projects are discontinued as early as possible. Someone should be made responsible for each project, so that the work is supervised and costs are kept within the agreed limits. There are a number of stages covered in controlling the projects and these are discussed below.

13.5.1   Project work programme

First a project work programme should be prepared by a project manager, showing:

1   The timing of the work to be done.
2   The materials, machinery, equipment and other facilities required, and the dates when each major item will be available.
3   The personnel required in terms of numbers, types, or grades,

and the dates when each must start.
4   The total costs expected at each stage of the project, and the anticipated progress, by dates.

In connection with this planning, it may be necessary to employ critical path networks, possibly using a computer, but where the projects are simple less sophisticated techniques may suffice. These would include detailed schedules, progress charts and timetables, to cover the main stages. These devices help to show what is expected, and represent the plans made. Subsequently, the actual achievements can be compared against various stages of the plan.

13.5.2   Progress reports

Each project can be the subject of control by preparing progress reports. These may be produced quarterly or at some other convenient time, depending on the nature of the project. Each report would show the following:

1   Progress made in relation to the timetable.
2   Achievements on the project and any technical difficulties experienced.
3   Costs incurred showing:
     a   actual costs
     b   budgeted costs;
     c   variances where appropriate.

These progress reports could be prepared on a standard form, and circulated in accordance with the procedures laid down within the system.

After the project has been running for some time, it will be necessary to reappraise the objectives to see whether there is justification for carrying on as originally planned. This reappraisal should be carried out at least once a year, but a more cursory inspection of the results could be carried out quarterly, when the progress report is prepared.

For a major project the reappraisal should be looked at by the committee which approved the project in the first place; would follow the points covered on the progress report. There may be circumstances where information is available to the committee which was not known by the project manager, and this may influence the committee on deciding whether or not a project should be abandoned or whether more effort should be put into it.

Tasks	Executive responsibility	Advisory committees	Staff support	Influence of outside depts
R&D objectives				
Formulation of telecommunications business objectives	Managing Director	Managing Director's Committee	Corporate planning	Membership of Man. Dir's Committee
Formulation of R&D objectives	R&D Director	R&D Review Committee		Membership of R&D Review Committee
Approval of R&D objectives	Managing Director	Man. Dir's Committee		Membership of Man. Dir's Committee
R&D projects				
Preparation of project proposals	R&D Director & senior managers	–		Submission of ideas for R&D projects
Preparation of project justification	Project managers	–	Mngt acctg	Provision of inform- ation for justification
Project evaluation	R&D Director	R&D Review Committee	Fncl plng	Membership of R&D Review Committee
Project approval & authorisation	Man. Dir. & R&D Director	R&D Review Committee	Corp plng	–
Project control: Routine Review Appraisal	Project Manager R&D Director	– – R&D Review Committee	Mngt acctg Fncl plng Corp plng	Receipt of project progress reports. Membership of R&D Review Committee
R&D programme				
Formulation of R&D programme	R&D Director	R&D Review Committee	Corporate planning Financial planning	Membership of R&D Review Committee
Approval of R&D programme	Managing Director	Man.Dir's Committee		Membership of Man. Dir's Committee

Figure 13.4 Organisation for R&D

Within an organisation there should be clearly defined lines of authority and responsibility, this can be done by preparing suitably drafted chart showing the following management responsibilities:

1   *Advisory functions* on the R&D corporate objectives and strategy. This function will probably be carried out by a committee which includes those from various functional areas who act in advisory capacities.
2   *Initiation and planning responsibility*   The types of projects, and the committee, or persons who can initiate projects, as well as the procedures, would be indicated in the organisation chart, or in a manual.
3   *Support from related departments*   The place of the accounting and other functional departments, such as corporate planning, should be shown so that each is aware of the part (it must) play in establishing the R&D objectives.

An indication of the development of the organisation is given in Figure 13.4. It is broken down into a number of sections as follows:

1   Objectives or tasks.
2   Responsibilities of directors and managers.
3   Advisory committees.
4   Related departments' support.
5   Coordination.

This chart can be varied to suit specific requirements, but its main purpose is to show at a glance who is responsible, and how the various aspects are coordinated, so that overlap is avoided.

13.7   ACCOUNTING SYSTEM

The accounting system adopted will depend upon a number of factors as outlined in Chapters 6, 8 and 13. The purpose would be to accumulate costs relating to research and development in such a way that the cost of individual projects could be seen, as well as the annual costs and variances from the allowances given in the budgets. There should be appropriate forms or statements to show:

1   What has been planned in terms of activity and cost.
2   The detailed cost for each project.

3   Reports and statements on the state of the project at the end of
     each control period.
4   A breakdown of any variances and the action to be taken.

For tracing costs and charging them to appropriate projects, there
should be a suitable coding system as well as material requisitions and
other authorisation forms showing what has been spent and by whom
authorised. When developing the system, care should be taken in
designing the forms and showing the flow of information – the
source, those responsible for its preparation, and those who will
receive the various forms or statements.
   A vital part of accounting for R&D will be the allocation of code
numbers, covering:

1   Accounts in the ledger.
2   Projects, distinguishing:
     a   those covering revenue expenditure within the period; and.
     b   capital expenditure, which is treated as a fixed asset and
            written off over a number of years.

In designing an accounts code, attention should be paid to all activity
areas which would be linked into a fully comprehensive coding
systen. As with all systems, the design should satisfy the specific
requirements of the business, and there should be no attempt to
produce a standard package to cover all circumstances.

14
R&D IN
PRACTICE

14.1   BACKGROUND RESEARCH

As part of the research for this book, many R&D establishments were
visited and facts were collected. In this chapter, a summarised version
of the organisation of research and development at British Petroleum
is given. This stresses the accounting requirements, but even these of
necessity have been kept brief. However, it is hoped that the outline
will at least give some idea of the complex structure required with an
international company of the size of BP.

Following that description are a number of very brief summaries
which include the main features of the organisation for research and
development in leading companies. Figures have not been included,
because these quickly become out of date, and would not reflect the
current activities of the business in question.

14.2   CASE STUDY 1: R&D AT BRITISH PETROLEUM

(Inevitably what follows is an historical account and changes which
have taken place since may require some modification of the description. However, the general principles still apply).

The bulk of the organised research is at Sunbury Research Centre,
which is a semi-autonomous cost centre within the research and
technical development department at BP. The centre also houses
laboratories, which are divisions of the exploration department and
of BP Chemicals Limited.

The organisation chart in Figure 14.1 shows the general organisation
of the research effort. This is followed by Figure 14.2, which indicates
the management relationships between the different sectors of the
business. It will be seen that these relationships are represented by
three types of line:

1   Executive Control – straight line.
2   Policy Control – dashed line.
3   Advisory and Consultative – dot/dash line.

The Research Centre is shown within the shaded area in Figure 14.2,
whereas outside that area are the various departments involved in the
R&D effort.

There are three main divisions within the main research centre –
the Petroleum, Exploration and Chemical Divisions. They concentrate
on the products and services which come within their broad responsibilities.

14.2.1   Outline of budgetary control

In July/August each year a financial cost budget is drafted, covering
the main divisions and branches. This has three main parts:-

1   *Establishment budget* – consisting of salaries and associated
     costs for personnel, and other normal recurring expenditure.
     This is based on the current staff establishment and any known
     or projected changes.
2   *General provisions* – a general sum is allocated for each unit to
     cover items such as cost of living increases, replacement of equip-
     ment (small items), redecorations.
3   *Special provisions* – This is an additional sum covering specific
     requirements of a special nature, such as large items of new or
     additional equipment, whether generally for a department or
     specifically for a project.

These items are summarised for each unit and division, and for the
Centre. The total budget is then considered by the General Manager
and forwarded to Head Office for approval. The total tends to remain
reasonably constant.

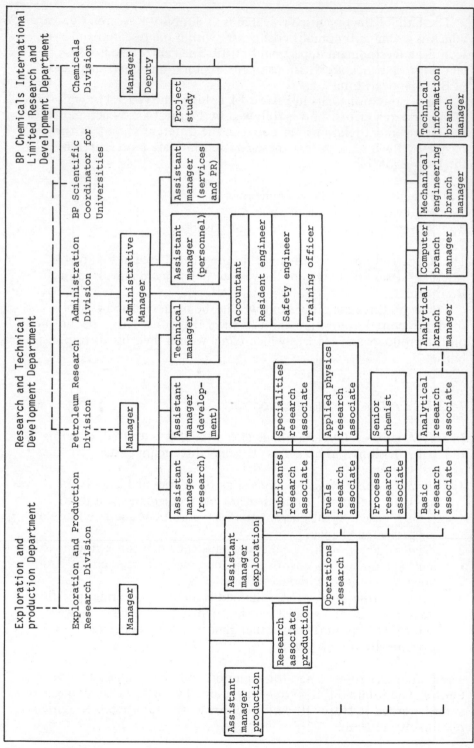

Figure 14.1 Organisation chart for BP Research Centre, Sunbury

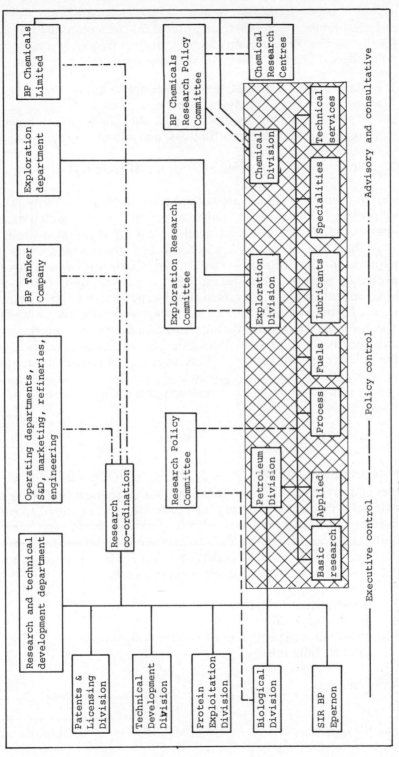

Figure 14.2 Organisation of BR research effort

—— Executive control   ——— Policy control   —·—·— Advisory and consultative

In September/October the technical research plans are considered, locally by the project teams then by project managers and policy committees. The research is divided approximately as follows:

1   *Basic research* — relatively low capital or human investment, and long time span of activity to achieve results.
2   *Applied research* — more directly associated with technical application of research findings, and solving practical commercial problems.
3   *Service work* — routine analytical and technical support.

Within each broad group are several general lines of activity, known as 'projects'. These are basically subject areas within which many lines of specific research and development are conducted ('jobs').

Technical effort is assessed in terms of technical man hours required for particular jobs (within project groups), which are expected to be undertaken during the year ahead. These technical man-hour budgets are not converted into financial terms. They are allocations of gross available time of staff who work directly on R&D activities, e.g. laboratory technicians. The hours used are the total number for which an individual is employed in the year, thus giving the number of staff required. This does not give the hours required for controlling time actually recorded.

The technical budgets are finally approved by the research policy committees.

14.2.2   Accounting

Expenditure commitments are recorded manually especially for special provisions. Cash payments are summarised monthly on a computer print-out. Outstanding commitments are added to produce a statement of monthly expenditure. This is given to each branch or unit manager, grouped by the three expenditure classifications, showing 'salaries', 'special provisions' and 'general provisions', with details of specific items. Information shown is:

1   Expenditure to date.
2   Budget for year.
3   Percentage expenditure of annual budget (compared with percent of time into year).

An example is:

	3 months to date	Budget	25%
Establishment	£2,400	£10,000	24%

This indicates that total expenditure is running slightly below budget.
Establishment expenditure is found to run fairly evenly throughout
the year. General provisions are available for balancing over and
under expenditures within a branch, or even between branches.

Special provisions are not necessarily committed evenly throughout the year. Watch is kept on the percentage of total commitment
to total budget.

The budget is managed as far as possible by keeping total expenditure within the overall budget for the centre. The responsibility
for this is delegated from the general manager to the administrative
manager and through him to the Accountant. Thus the basic method
of control is to authorise an overall cash outlay within the budget
sums.

A quarterly and annual summary of expenditure is prepared and
circulated to head office. This shows expenditure incurred by the
various functions (or divisions) and an allocation to the various areas
of research. The method of allocation is described later. (Costing of
time spent on projects).

A further summary is prepared for the purpose of integrating costs
by types of expenditure into head office accounting. This is coordinated by coding all expenditure by expense analysis codes required by Head Office, e.g. salaries, rent, rates, development expenditure. This is not used by Sunbury Research Centre.

14.2.3 Project costs

The financial budget is based on types of expenditure to be incurred
by the various laboratories and branches, but not by projects and
jobs within projects.

Time budgeted to be spent on projects is based on the total hours
per man year (1950). Hours to be recorded against jobs will be less,
because of known absence, e.g. holidays and sickness. Actual hours
spent on jobs (which are numbered) are recorded monthly by the
three grades of staff (graduate technologists, technicians, assistants).
A computer report is issued showing:-

Hours spent this period
Cumulative hours to date
Budgeted hours for year
Net effective bookable hours
(Budgeted hours reduced for standard allowance for holidays,
etc.) Percentage use of actual hours compared to time expired
proportion of net budgeted hours.

This time report is made available to project managers quarterly, or more frequently as required, or as deemed necessary by the Administrative or Technical Managers. The Technical Manager's assistant plots the hours recorded in graph form to compare with budgets, and can thus advise the Technical Manager when work recorded is departing from budget.

These time reports provide a basis for discussion at regular technical progress meetings.

14.2.4 Costing of time spent on projects

Each branch or laboratory budget consists of all costs which can be directly associated therewith. These are divided into three groups according to the technical staff grades, and costing rates are thus produced. The time recorded is costed at these rates for the financial cost reports, which are broken down into job detail.

The detailed quarterly financial reports are produced from these costings, and are seen as a financial measure of the effort spent on each job, but are not used for planning or budgetary control. This provides a simple method of controlling effort by time, and ensures that financial problems are segregated from the scientific at the lower levels of responsibility.

It is deemed that financial control is the responsibility of the general technical and administrative managers, but that scientific effort should be controlled separately.

No attempt is made to link the financial and time budgets, except to ensure that the same staff are included in each. Financial budgets are not prepared for projects or jobs.

A project study group attached to Head Office has been established to examine the possibility of quantifying future costs and anticipated benefits with a view to using this information to assist Research Planning managers and the project study group to make better advised decisions as to allocation of funds.

14.2.5 Accounting procedures

There now follows an outline of the accounting procedures used in BP together with specimen operating statements.

Summary of Accounting Procedures

The Project Costs summarise the effort, measured in technical man-hours and expenditure, on Research Projects.

1 BASIC DATA

Capital expenditure

Requests for capital indicate the projects with which they are associated. The totals of the capital releases thus associated are shown against each project.

The allocation of technical man-hours to projects includes an estimate of time to be spent on associated capital work by the Mechanical Engineering Branch technical staff. To provide comparable figures, it has been necessary to include the man-hours actually spent on associated capital work in the 'man-hours expended' figure. The cost of these hours, which was included in the Capital release, is not included in the revenue expenditure.

Revenue expenditure

Revenue expenditure may be directly or indirectly associated with a project. Indirect expenditure, or overhead, as it is generally described, is that which cannot reasonably be allocated directly to a particular project, e.g. management expenditure, general plant or building maintenance, engineering services, utilities and site administration. The collection of revenue expenditure uses an eight-digit code representing division, branch and project or overhead allocation. Copies of revenue expenditure allocation codes are distributed to branch/project managements who are responsible for the control of expenditure within approved financial budgets.

(a) *Salaries* Staff are classified as Technical (Technologists and Assistants) and Non-technical, and the amounts allocated to projects are the product of man-hours and average salary rates (including housing subsidies, pensions, graduated pensions and National Insurance contributions) for each classification within projects and branches.

(b) *Other costs* Expenditure allocations are made by requisitionists. The correctness of allocations is the responsibility of those authorising the expenditure, but is also scrutinised by Accounts.

(c) *Engineering services* The total cost of the Mechanical Engineering Branch is allocated to projects and to capital by means of a 'Job costing' system. Each job is associated with a project or capital budget, with the exception of the jobs originated by MEB for supervision, consumables and workshop overheads. The expenditure on these overhead jobs is distributed by means of an on-cost to the salary rate per hour, charged to jobs. In addition, site expenses and division overheads associated with MEB are included in the Engineering Services charged to projects on the basis of their use of the engineering services.

(Continued overleaf)

The salaries of technical staff completing time sheets
are excluded and appear in 'Salaries' in order that salary
costs may be compared with the programmed technical man-hours.

(d) Division overheads Division overheads are allocated
first to branches by means of the technical strengths, and
then to projects on the basis of technical man-hours booked
to projects by the Branch.

(e) Site services For the sake of simplicity and, because
other methods give almost identical results, the cost of
site services is allocated to projects on a man-power basis.

Items of site service expenditure, which are not necessarily allocable on the basis of man-power, in particular the
utilities, are carefully checked each year to ensure that
changing circumstances do not invalidate the present arbitrary
allocation. It should be pointed out that, without metering
the services to each project, any method of allocation is, of
necessity, somewhat arbitrary.

An allocation is first made to the Branches on the basis
of total strength within each Branch, and then to projects
on the basis of total man-hours (Technical and Non-technical)
booked to projects by the Branches.

2 REALLOCATIONS

(a) Supporting research and development of methods

The 200 series projects. This expenditure is reallocated to
Applied and Fundamental Research Projects in proportion to
the estimated benefits which each has gained.

(b) Miscellaneous Technical Services

The 300 series projects. The majority of this expenditure is
reallocated to Applied and Fundamental Research Projects.

(c) Third-party work - non-recoverable

Projects in the 775-799 series and Project 529. Non-
recoverable costs are reallocated to Applied and Fundamental Research Projects.

(d) Third-party work - recoverable

Projects in the 500 series. Costs of recoverable third-party
work are not reallocated, but where the work was included
in the Project programme, the recoverable expenditure is
included in the total cost of the project.

Research and Technical Development Department: Research Division

Project costs summary: Statement 1

Title	Total direct[1]		Total including overheads[2]		Total including reallocations[3]		Capital amount released £	Total including reallocations		Capital amount released £
	Technical man-hours	£	Technical man-hours	£	Technical man-hours	£		Technical man-hours	£	
Applied research projects										
Fundamental research projects										
Supporting research and development of methods										
Technical services to Services Division										
Technical services to other divisions										
Miscellaneous technical services										
Non-recoverable work for third parties										
Recoverable work for third parties										
TOTAL EFFORT ON RESEARCH PROJECTS										
Capital releases - unallocated to projects										

[1] Direct technical man-hours are comparable with project allocations
[2] Overheads include Division and Branch overheads, with administration site services
[3] Reallocations include supporting research, technical service work and non-recoverable work for third parties

Research and Technical Development Department: Research Division

Project costs summary: Statement 1 (detail)

Project title	Technical man-hours			Salaries		Mater-ials	Contr-acts	Sund-ries	Engin-eering Services	Division Over-heads	Site ser-vices	Total revenue expenditure	Capital released 19--
	Allocation	Expended		Tech.Staff inc. MEB tech.staff	Non-tech. staff								
		By R&TD Div.	By R&DD Divs										
	hr	hr	hr	£	£	£	£	£	£	£	£	£	£
Applied research projects													
Fundamental research projects													
Supporting research and development of methods													
Technical services to services div.													
Technical services to other divs													
Miscellaneous technical services													
Recoverable work for third parties													
Non-recoverable work for third parties													
Capital releases - unallocated to projects													

Research and Technical Development Department: Research Division: Project Costs: Statement 3

Division/Branch Overheads	Tech man-hours	£	Administration Site Services (Research Project share)	£
Branch overheads (expenditure which cannot be directly allocated to a project)			*Personnel services*	
Management			Passenger transport	
Analytical Branch			Medical	
Basic research projects			Welfare	
Process projects			Catering	
A projects			Staff Club	
Applied physics projects			Sports events	
B projects			*Main stores expenses*	
C projects			*Site expenses*	
Technical Information Branch			Site upkeep	
Overhead projects (incl. MEB overheads, man-hours only)			Fire, security and safety	
Project 401 Staff training in research centre			*Utilities*	
402			Steam service	
.			Electrical service	
.			.....	
422 Inter-Centre Conference			.....	
Abstract services			*Building Maintenance (General administration)*	
Research Institute - Long-range planning servce			General administration staff services	
Telepr			Despatch service	
Engineering services			Public relations	
Less Transfer to MEB			Accounts, Insurance, Training	
Own technical effort for associated projects			*Sub Stores expenses*	
Add Associated Division effort for own projects			SITE SERVICES BASED ON OWN EFFORT	
Research projects share			*Less* Own technical effort for associated projects	
ENGINEERING SERVICES			*Add* Associated Division effort for own projects	
Direct costs			SITE SERVICES BASED ON TOTAL EFFORT ON OWN PROJECTS	
Less Salaries of programmed technical staff				
Associated Division overheads				
Associated site services				
Research projects share				

Research Centre: Functional Analysis of Revenue Expenditure

Statement 3

	Research, fundamental, applied & supporting research projects £	Associated research projects £	Production research £	Technical development £	Biological research £	Misc. technical services to group £	Recoverable expenditure £	Total £
Research Division (excluding Mechanical Engineering Branch)								
Mechanical Engineering Branch								
Administration Division								
Production Research Division								
Technical Development Division								
Associated Division								

To:	Technical Manager		Date:	
From:	Accountant, BP Research Centre			
Subject:	Revenue expenditure, January 19--			

GROSS BUDGET	Budget, 19--, £	Actual £'s expenditure	Percentage of year	Project actual, 19--, £
Salaries				
Special provisions				
General provisions				
Research, Kent				
Recoverable				
TOTAL				

AVERAGE STRENGTH	Budget, 19--	January, 19--
Technologists		
Assistants		
Clerical, etc.		
Supervision		
Craftsmen, Operators, etc.		

GENERAL PROVISIONS	Provision	Actual expenditure	Percentage of year
Analytical branch			
Basic research projects			
Process projects			
Fuels projects			
Applied physics projects			
Lubricants projects			
Specialities projects			
Mechanical Engineering Branch			
Technical Information Branch			
Divisional Management and secondments			

SPECIAL PROVISIONS	Allocation number	Description	Provision £	Expenditure & commitments £

Company: a large electronics group that is a leader in its field.

14.3.1 Procedures

The company has a divisionalised organisation structure, for groups, or areas of operations. Each division covers a range of product lines and has its own R&D department; the divisions operate as separate businesses, having individual budgets and accounts. Their R&D is primarily product development, engineering services and technical services for customer systems. There is a central R&D unit covering fundamental research. Each division undertakes long-range planning on a formal basis.

Project selection, evaluation and continuous audit are subject to formal procedures, but there are no standardised proposal forms or planning procedures due to the diversity of product range over all divisions.

The central technical administration unit provides a team of R&D administrators to collect data, prepare budgets and monitor projects, within divisions and at central office to coordinate financial control.

14.3.2 Budgetary control

Divisional budgets are related to the cash flow of divisions but where necessary additional R&D finance is permitted despite operational losses, in order not to jeopardise an existing programme or new worthwhile projects.

Technical assistance is provided for sales and tender work, and R&D also covers adaptive engineering.

There is an overall budget for R&D embracing all divisions, which is compiled monthly, consolidating all divisional budgets, vetting out interdivisional research work. The budgets for divisions carry materials, labour and overheads, the latter covering heat, light, services and depreciation absorbed on a labour hour basis.

14.5.3 Control

There are regular meetings of production, sales, marketing and R&D staff, for project proposals. These are evaluated, and staff making estimates must sign the proposal form and accept responsibility for their estimates. The latter are not probabilistic. The proposal form goes to the divisional manager who can authorise projects and go ahead, but no work can be commenced until an engineering order is placed for the project. At this point Central Technical Administration provides booking numbers for data collection against the project.

Booking numbers are not given until all the factors for consideration have been examined and decisions made thereon. A check list of factors covers manpower available, timing, compatibility and existing product line, and capital expenditure requirements.

Accuracy of technical estimates is high and this is built into the evaluation process. Different minimum criterion rates are employed for various projects and divisions, which must be equated or exceeded on evaluation.

Resource scheduling is done by a detailed plan for each research man showing the manhours required for each project. A minimal slack is allowed between his completion and start of projects. If, due to inadequacy in scheduling time completion for a task, a succeeding project is delayed, the excess time on the preceding project is recorded as a penalty against that product group managers' budget. Over-generous estimating like all estimates, being measured in money terms, means the cost of the proposal would militate against its selection unless benefits were sufficient to compensate the extra cost.

Risk analysis is not employed, so the tendency is for single figure estimates to be obtained.

Some projects are 'PERTed' — in which case R&D personnel compile the PERT networks. Monthly budgets are prepared for product groups and variances are fully investigated. Gantt bar charts show planned and actual progress over project stages, updated to show early on where divergencies occur.

Proposal estimates for stages in money terms are placed on the project Gantt chart, actuals to-date are given, as are cumulative figures that which can be compared with the estimated total project cost.

Progress completion can be expressed in terms of cumulative expenditure divided into total-project estimated cost as a percentage. Committed costs are shown, to complete the financial data. Reviews take place when any of the stages are overrun, per month, or when the project is near satisfactory completion, or when a slight tendency for actual costs to exceed planned costs is indicated. A major review occurs when cumulative costs exceed the estimated project total cost, before project completion, but usually this tendency is spotted in stage cost overrun.

For review purposes, total actual and committed costs to-date are regarded as the maximum loss in the event of project rejection.

The entire system is computerised. Divisional R&D budgets comprise product group budgets which include the Gantt chart, budgets and actuals for projects, all prepared on a monthly basis. Consequently variances can be traced down to projects for casual factors.

14.4   CASE STUDY 3: A LARGE PHARMACEUTICAL COMPANY

Company: A large pharmaceutical company with interests in many countries, but primarily in the UK and the USA.

14.4.1   Corporate plan

The plan coordinates research into compounds, chemicals and processes, together their development stages both for the UK and America. There is a three-year plan covering total company objectives involving R&D, marketing, production, and diversification, again for the UK and American activities.

14.4.2   Budgetary control

About 12 to 15 per cent of the total R&D budget goes on basic research on projects concerned with extant compound analysis, the stabilisation of chemical break-down in shelf life and production terms, toxicity studies and testing as well as searching for new knowledge. The availability of animals for toxicity tests and their duration to meet new drug regulations operates as a resource constraint. These tests precede clinical tests, shelf-life tests and tests on appropriate methods of drug administration. According to type, new drugs can take three to five years before reaching the market.

Uncertainties are great. Of 3000 new formulations only one or two may be commercially successful. There does not appear to be a capital-rationing constraint explicitly in that all market areas and proposals considered worthy of R&D effort are pursued, but often manpower constraints operate to require a re-allocation over projects. The R&D unit was established almost 20 years ago and has grown steadily, but now has reached an optimum size. But this company like all other firms interviewed, did not know and had not attempted to study, what was an optimum size R&D unit. It appears that the size of the budget was such that is would prove difficult to authorise more. In the past, success has brought requests for, and approval of, increased budgets.

Project budget aggregation plus a fixed percentage for cost increase is the method used for R&D budget requests. In three years hence,

greater testing resources will be required for compounds currently
emerging from research studies — and it is this compound research-
test cycle that fixed the corporate planning horizon at three years.
Networking — without uncertainty or risk probabilities — is used for
process engineering, but not for product R&D projects, which contain at most, 150 activities.

14.4.2   Techniques employed

Informal evaluation is used within executive project management
teams. There is no standard format for proposals, but each proposal
is examined for a list of conditions to apply. No formal checklist or
procedures are used. Project selection is by committee comprising
heads of R&D departments. There are seven research disciplines,
which are inter-mixed on project work. Marketing, production and
R&D functions have been recently brought in for corporate planning
and project selection purposes, but new product initiation comes
from R&D rather than marketing. Projects are reviewed monthly
against budgets, by R&D department heads, not by project leaders.
  There are no OR scientists employed for optimising techniques.
The project selection panel meets quarterly, but are largely
governed by the American company's corporate strategy — meetings
in America take place annually.
  Resource-scheduling is a major problem embracing research manpower, but particularly, testing facilities. 'PERTing' and resource-
scheduling are computerised. Project data will be next for computer
application.

14.5   CASE STUDY 4: PART OF AN INTERNATIONAL GROUP

Company: Part of an international group operating throughout the
world, primarily as manufacturers of electrical and domestic products.

14.5.1   Notion of research and development

In this division of the group research is separate from development in
terms of:

1   Organisation.
2   Resources of manpower, equipment, building and finance.
3   Policy and objectives.

There are specifically three activities:

a   Fundamental research.
b   Multi-use of components.
c   Component or materials development, e.g. integrated circuit or
    semi-conductor development.

14.5.2   Fundamental research

This is managed by a research director responsible for resource
planning, budgeting and some control. There is a long-term budget
which comes from a central pool, itself generated by past profits.
The budget is reviewed periodically within the year and in detail at
the year-end.
   Selection criteria are as follows:

1   *Areas of work*   Two broad categories of materials or
    components.
2   *Project selection*   Dependent upon the individual research
    worker, to make a convincing case covering:
    a   relevancy and need for the project;
    b   resources of commitment required;
    c   methods of tackling the problem;
    d   time-scale for approximate results, usually on a stage-by-
        stage process.

Resources include composition of the teams, equipment, space and
financial elements incorporated into a planned programme.
   Vetting procedures depend on the resource commitment required.
Department heads and the director of research, both experienced in
vetting projects and research methodology, decide from competing
projects, those most suitable for the current programme.
   Essentially, research men are not discouraged. If several competing
projects emerge, the budget will be enlarged if necessary. Projects that
require a large commitment of resources are vetted by service management at group HQ.
   The background of the project proposer is known, his specialisms,
strengths and weaknesses, and past successes. If he is new, he is encouraged to take a major work load in a team project he originates.
There is interdependence of projects, interchange of research staff
and continuous liaison throughout the group.
   Classified work accounts for about 30 per cent of all fundamental
research – this proportion is maintained as a top management policy.
A greater proportion would mean interference with company objec-

tives, whilst too little may lower staff morale and long-term competency. The company passes on expertise in specific research areas, is usually approached by Government agencies for cooperation, and receives sound theoretical advice and facilities. Projects are financed on a 50-50 basis — the company and the parent company. Company policy is to welcome projects to maintain or improve the research competence of staff, to maintain staff morale, and to foster good relations with government agencies.

Occasionally, when project work if declassified a commercial product may emerge. All classified work is embraced within the fundamental research organisation, the only special requirements being for security procedures on documents and use of research buildings.

Projects are planned and long-range budgeting proposals for the projects must have an appearance of viability, but control of projects is loose. Research staff are conscious of the need for appropriate spheres of work within the confines of company products, but cost-consciousness is not enforced, there being a deliberate policy of freedom to choose research methods and individuality of project choice.

Progress reports are called for and stage scheduling encouraged to identify those phases with *greater* problems. Probable outcomes are not evaluated, nor are benefits, either directly related to projects or spin-off. The latter levels do benefit the industry — the parent company encourages publication of their results.

Benefits accrue to the company's leadership in specific areas, which attracts research recruits, creates better markets and provides opportunities for classified work. Time-lags are long range, thus creating difficulties for benefit measurement. Opportunity cost notions are considered inapplicable.

14.5.3 Applications

Development work is done on components or materials which can be used in several different products.

Selection of projects is determined by market intelligence, consumer use and the desire to improve technological performance. Examples are standardisation of components, improving the reliability of circuitry and microminiaturisation applications.

Planning and control procedures are rigorously applied to development programmes, but evaluation of benefits is difficult to quantify due to multi use of project results over product groups, in the home and overseas manufacturing plants.

Projects are selected as a matter of routine, based on full analysis from market research, production or modification specifications, and from market intelligence on competitors' products.

Projects are fully planned, with PERT scheduling, manhour allocation, equipment use, space and materials. Production control, work study, O&M and other relevant services are used by development engineers and scientists. Development laboratories are part of the production plants.

Pay-off ratings are used on a quasi-probability rating for planning and costing data.

Budgetary control is used rigorously for all projects together with detailed costing and variance analysis. These procedures are feasible due to technical knowledge and experience of the product type.

Time is of the essence, and once a project is scheduled the schedule is rarely changed even if competitors launch competing developments, since acceleration of project work entails reallocation of equipment, space and manpower resources, the latter being expensive and difficult to obtain readily.

The market structure is such that development work will find a place, especially when production volume brings down price. Very rarely, projects are written off prior to completion.

Development work and project selection operates by routine processes, but experience shows that *ad hoc* project teams, fully committed and specially chosen, work more economically than workers on routine project work programmes.

14.6   CASE STUDY 5: A LEADING MANUFACTURING AND MARKETING GROUP

Company: a leading group manufacturing and marketing a wide range of earthenware, sanitary ware and plastic products.

14.6.1   Main research areas

The Research Company has four main areas of work:

1   *Chemistry and mineralogy* maintains analysis of raw materials for quality control, materials development, competitors' products, and technical troubleshooting for manufacturing and customer queries. Process control is involved in quality control of finished product and intermediate processes, e.g. glazing and refiring.

2   *Materials development* is concerned with specific composition
     for industrial and consumer application, e.g. improved hardness,
     tensile, ductile strengths, bonding to metal and changing
     viscosity for improving pressings of tableware and processing.
3   *The plastics* area covers substitute material for outdoor use,
     lightweight materials, resin and bonding problems and plastici-
     sers for glazing and ceramic bonding.
4   *The engineering area* contains three functions: design of machines,
     kilns, process-plant and moulding machines, and essentially
     assists R&D by ensuring that products/prototypes are capable of
     satisfactory performance, cost, and manufacture parameters,
     prior to large scale commitment of resources. Design of product,
     process and equipment are involved in this liaison; for example,
     sanitary ware comprises yellow coarse earthenware, which is
     fired, then coated with a hard white substance, glazed and
     refired. A project, consuming two/three years' work, and con-
     siderable resources was devoted to developing a white earthen-
     ware which hardened white on a once-off firing. This was
     achieved, but never incorporated in a product, since to do so
     would have involved major changes in production methods and
     factory location, and a huge investment of finance. On a cost-
     benefit analysis, this was not feasible, despite an obvious
     technical success. Engineering liaison is meant to overcome this
     problem. The other two functions are development of machines,
     processes and hardware 'pieces' for adaptation of machines or
     development of novel devices using 'off the shelf' components.

The four research areas are primarily concerned with development
work, only one long-term, small project being admitted to a programme comprising about twenty projects on average. This project
concerns technological forecasting, to find substitute material for
bone china in ten years' time. A substitute has been found, but is too
expensive for current usage.

14.6.2   Development of R&D

The research unit has been in existence for 15 years and currently
has staff of 45 including technicians and clerical staff, but formalised
procedures, organisation liaison, managerial objectives and product-
rationalisation, have only come into use in the last few years.

There is one 'O&M' function which comprises at present industrial
engineering, but may take in OR in the near future (trouble-shooting).

Historically the research function was established to provide company growth. This was to be achieved by product rationalisation, cost

reduction schemes in manufacture and innovating new products and processes. Earthenware/sanitaryware is technically problematical, highly competitive and provides small profit margins. Their production processes are still fraught with a large degree of technical risk. Earthenware sewer pipes, a large part of the business, has been sold off. Tableware is highly profitable, but only recently has been automated to lower production costs. Industrial products and plastics as a recent addition, provide a need for innovation, are profitable, but comprise a relatively small growing part of revenue.

The great majority of research time has been taken up with technical troubleshooting to the detriment of product and process development, and long-term research in particular. Associated companies in the group, are charged for these services to mitigate their impact on the research programme. Industrial engineering services are also charged out. Technical directors (ex-research company) of associated companies, the Group MD and Research Manager meet bimonthly to review project progress. Company objectives are set for each year, with participation of associated companies and R&D representatives. Projects ideally stem from three sources

1   Top company policy-objectives.
2   Recommendations of OR study team.
3   Developments of engineering services.

The emphasis is to move towards (1) and (2) where (2) would adopt a systems approach to areas of investigation, specialisms required, design for performance and for production, which is compatible with R&D programme balance, company resources and objectives. Systems engineering will probably play a large role in project specification.

14.6.3   Procedures

Project-teams are a loose amalgam of specialisms, personnel changing from project to project, often working in more than one team.

There is no capital rationing constraint in explicit form – all project ideas, within objectives, usually aim to meet a known need, and are commenced subject to manpower availability. Evaluation forms are used, and for large, complex projects, CPA networks have been used. Hart's discounting chart, a check-list of project elements and risk analysis are used – dependent on the project-complexity. (For an explanation of Hart's chart, which is used in comparing the relative merits of new products, see [11].)

Manpower scheduling is done over projects and time, to allow flexibility of movement from one project to another. Project budgeting is loose — according to the estimated man-days on the evaluation form. Actual man-days and costs are analysed over project and function on a bi-weekly basis, for review meetings.

Project leaders fill out a standard form, to show progress, anticipated and cumulative costs and technical difficulties. Capital expenditure required for a project must be shown — but not estimates for innovation expenditure likely to result if the project outcome is successful. It appears that the marketing requirements are only consulted indirectly unless the technical directors embrace the marketing requirements. Further, the Research Company is not represented on the Group Board, but the Group Managing Director and Chariman do sit on the Company's Research Board.

Gantt charts are frequently used to display current/historical progress of all projects — yet the estimated time, and costs over stages, compared with their actuals, are not shown. Nor are committed costs. Gantt charts are used for manpower schedules with similar shortcomings.

A technical committee comprising technical directors, Group MD and Research Manager meet bi-monthly for project review and to test achievement of objectives against targets in objectives. They can and do execute policy and make changes to the R&D emphasis, programme balance and manpower allocation.

Project idea generation, selection, control and manpower scheduling are adequate for this size company, but become rapidly misleading and inadequate as R&D programme balance changes, and product range moves from risk areas to uncertainty areas.

Capital-rationing is implicit in terms of the alternative use of R&D resources, and their servicing, and explicit in terms of the R&D manpower constraint, yet there is no current 'backlog' of projects. This may change as the R&D programme balance moves away from technical troubleshooting, (involving no project or evaluation heirarchy) to R&D projects, and some long-term research. Different skills and procedures may then be requested.

14.6.4 Type of work produced

A typical machine innovation from the engineering area is a quasi-injection moulding machine for production of ceramic lavatory cisterns. Use is made of hydraulic power (oil and water) and electricity for the motor supply. The design makes extensive use of 'off the shelf components' to give reliability, cheapness and availability of component parts. Thus the machine represents 'innovation through adaptation' of standard components used in other, more familiar applications. It requires original thinking in design. Advantages are in quantity production, reduced cost and increased reliability.

Only one purpose-made component is incorporated – a filter for separation of water and oil in the hydraulic system – a 'fail safe' device. Banks of four machines can be controlled by one operator from a central console, thus saving manpower and giving consistent quality.

Systems engineering design may have meant designing all components into an integrated machine concept, creating a more compact machine, but requiring greater resource investment and more uncertainty in performance and reliability.

14.7 CASE STUDY 6: AN INTERNATIONAL DRUGS AND COSMETICS GROUP

Company: a drugs and cosmetic group of international standing which has diversified its range of products considerably in the last decade.

14.7.1 General organisation

There are twenty projects ongoing in any year, of which four are devoted to long-term objectives. About 25 per cent of projects are defensive to up-date products, or bring in new technology into re-formulation of extant products.

The great majority of work is OTC work comprising non-ethical non-prescription drugs and cosmetics with a pharmaceutical base. The latter include anti-allergy properties. The French, African and German market areas, including the UK, are strong – African for cosmetics, German for vitamin products, French for non-ethical liver drugs, or palliatives. A British-based firm, it is strong in present or former Commonwealth countries, e.g. India and Pakistan, and the Continent, but very weak in North and South America and absent from the Middle East.

14.7.2 Long-range planning

R&D staff are employed on development work on a main project and a subsidiary one, to facilitate changes of emphasis or success, from the main project, and prevent staleness. Marketing and technical development are integrated, but are operationally controlled by separate functional directors, under a managing director. Technical staff work under project leaders, who have full responsibility up to the pilot production run; thereafter a marketing project leader takes responsibility, with the technical leader retained in the team for experience of commercial exploitation and trouble-shooting and to provide consultative technical opinion. Project leaders can be very young and have a fairly free hand in choice of team. All development projects are networked using computer PERT and DCF techniques. Market research and marketing staff at home and abroad provide a full brief for filling customer-needs, competitors activities and new technologies. Technical intelligence is provided to back-up market research and marketing projects. New products require extensive advertising and judicial packaging for separate markets, the launch requiring heavy financial commitment for about two years to achieve satisfactory consumer acceptance. Product lives vary but often reach ten years without much modification. Development projects must show a break-even returns pattern within two years, usually 18 months. Rigorous technical and commercial feasibility studies precede development proposals – submitted to a 'Projects Committee' responsible for project selection and comprising LRP technical, research and operational-group heads, meeting quarterly for new projects, project review, merger/acquisition proposals and financial review. The LRP work is the full-time responsibility of one of the two executive directors; three-year corporate plans are detailed with acquisition, R&D and marketing strategies worked out for the International and European Divisions, across pharmaceuticals-Ethical-, OTC toiletries and cosmetics.

The present structure of LRP Technical and Commercial Development, and formal growth strategies is only seven years old. Until 19XX the firm was a one-product company. Major changes have resulted from fundamental issues concerning Ethical versus OTC products and the issue of pharmaceuticals or toiletries, cosmetics and similar, allied product fields. Considerable marketing strength has come via acquisitions, especially in overseas territories. One major problem now is the need to view operational activities along geographical market divisions rather than product divisions. This is the effect of variability from one country to another in acceptance of products – the Latin requirements of Spain, Italy, Portugal are different from France which is different from Germany, all of which are different from the UK and it and they are different from Scandinavian requirements. The complexities these variable-demand situations create has been countered largely by acquisitions, but the digestion of these is now beginning to create excessive demands on R&D and its commercial development. The latter also relies on a formal management development programme to train R&D staff in techniques of administration, decision-making, commercial orientation – a commitment made necessary to induce graduates to enter industry rather than stay on at University for higher-degree work.

The R&D staff is 50 strong, and total R&D budget figures are determined by project aggregation, in terms of LRP and corporate development plans. For example, a new product need, or product range can be provided from internal R&D provided the company has adequate marketing power to launch the innovation when required. If the latter point is dubious, then company acquisitions may supersede internal R&D as a vehicle of corporate growth.

14.10   CONCLUSION

The case studies given above should indicate that there is no standardised policy or procedures which can be applied within a business. Each company must be treated separately with its own special problems. The organisation, administration and financial control should give sufficient stimulus for creative work within a budget the business can afford.

REFERENCES

Many books and journals were referred to during the research for this book. Thanks are offered to the authors/editors, especially to the following mentioned in the text:

1   E. Duer Reeves, *Management of Industrial Research*, pp. 45-52, Rheinhold Corp., New York (1967).

2   T. S. McCleod, *Management of Research and Development, and Design in Industry*, p. 207, The Camelot Press, London (1969).

3   R. E. Seiler, *Improving the Effectiveness of Research and Development*, McGraw-Hill (1965).

4   B. V. Carsberg, *Introduction to Mathematical Programming for Accountants*, George Allen & Unwin, London (1969).

5   Management Accounting Practices Committee of the National Association of Accountants (USA), 'The capitalisation of costs as opposed to charging the cost off as an expense', *Management Accounting* (July 1972).

6   C. Stafforth (Editor), *Project Cost Control Using Networks*, Operational Research Society/Institute of Cost and Management Accountants, London (1969).

7   K. E. Rose, *Programme Budgeting*, Institute of Municipal Treasurers and Accountants (1969).

8   D. Novick, *Programme Budgeting*, Holt Reinhart & Winston, (Second edition, 1968).

9   A. H. Marshall, *Financial Management in Local Government*, George Allen & Unwin (1974).

10 D. R. Snyder, 'Cost analysis and control of RDT and E projects', *Management Accounting (USA)* (September 1971).

11 A. Hart, 'A chart for evaluating product research and development products', *Operational Research* Quarterly, **17**(4), pp. 347-358 (1966).

INDEX

Randall Library – UNCW
HF5681.R35 B37 1976
Batty / Accounting for research and development   NXWW

304900234529+